Rudy Vallée

A Pict ____ graphy

Doris Bickford-Swarthout

Foreword

My introduction to Rudy Vallée was the result of a chance reading of *Let the Chips Fall*. I knew who he was, of course, but little else. When the book was finished, I found I was feeling rather ambivalent toward the author — but, nevertheless, intrigued enough to want to see how biographers treated him. It was astounding to find out that there were no biographies, authorized or otherwise. This seemed hardly possible, as most show business legends are written about to death.

So the seed was sown and this is the result. I have not recounted all Rudy's many love affairs or feuds. He did that very well in his own "tell-all" books.

But no one ever tells all. My objective was to present Rudy as I discovered him and, more importantly, to remember a fabulous life and career.

Rudy was certainly an enigma — some co-workers adored him and others frankly disliked him. In the end I found that this multi-talented man was indeed difficult and certainly egotistical, but also loving and surprisingly generous. He was one-of-a-kind and, taken all together, a very decent human being.

Published in the USA by:
BearManor Media
P O Box 71426
Albany, Georgia 31708
www.bearmanormedia.com

ISBN 1-59393-140-9

Printed in the United States of America.

Book & cover design by Darlene and Dan Swanson of Van-garde Imagery, Inc.

Acknowledgements

A biography is written only with the cooperation and encouragement of a vast number of people. They are the generous ones, who will recount personal memories, share photos and give interviews. I appreciate them all, including folks who preferred to remain anonymous, but nevertheless gave interesting perspectives.

First, I want to thank Eleanor Vallée, who was originally apprehensive about my project. Once reassured about my goal, she was gracious and helpful.

To Douglas Swarthout, whose computer skills made pulling the book together possible. Also, he gave me access to his extensive collection of movie memorabilia.

Kylie Althouse-Pierce, for her excellent photography and her patience through it all in dealing with a "computer dummy."

Arthur Pierce, for making available hundreds of hours of tapes of Rudy's radio shows and remotes.

Chris Widomski, for skillfully transferring photos.

Raymond Wood, President of the Kate Smith Commemorative Society, for insight into the Vallée/Smith relationship.

Frank Bresee, for providing interviews and photos.

Donna Conley and Suzan Norton, of the Westbrook Historical Society, for photos, newspaper clippings and personal memories.

Island Pond, Vermont Historical Society for photos.

Brenda Howitson Steeves, Special Collections Department, Raymond Folger Library, University of Maine.

Mark McCormick, CPO, United States Coast Guard Library, for a loan of photos and tapes.

Ed Colbert for photos.

Christine Windhauser, Western Union archives, for supplying history of the first singing telegram.

Chuck Thompson, for photos and great personal memories.

Richard Finegan, for material on *Campus Sweethearts*.

Harry A. Freidenberg, for photos and interesting anecdotes.

John Wilkes (whose late sister-in-law organized Rudy's first fan club), for sharing photos and fan club memorabilia.

Museum of Television and Radio, Reference Department, N.Y., New York Public Library, Theatre Collection Division.

For comments, commentaries and encouragement, special thanks to Alan Young, Phyllis Diller, Rose Marie, Lucie Arnaz, Robert Goulet, Julius LaRosa, Mary Healy, Ann Miller and especially a lovely phone call from Fay Wray.

I am grateful also to all those unknown photographers whose works through the years have become prized parts of so many private collections and particularly to those collectors who willingly shared their treasures.

Contents:

Illustrations

Maine. They would remain there for nearly five years. Rudy recalled the bridge and Falls and his precarious adventures climbing above both. Other than that, the place was barely noted in his memoirs.

Rudy was eight years old and sister Kathleen four years older when the family made one more move. They settled at Westbrook, Maine, then a small town on the Presumpscot River. Charles Vallée, a pharmacist, began working for the C.B. Woodman drugstore. Several years later the store became part of the Rexall chain and Vallée became the sole proprietor.

A one-year-old future crooner

Rudy, as a 6-year-old, already displaying that determined look

Rudy's memories of the drugstore were bittersweet. Charles was determined that his eldest son would become a pharmacist and join him in his business. The young boy had chores to do before breakfast that would have crushed a lesser spirit. Going into the drugstore basement, his early morning job, whatever the season, was to chop buckets of ice to keep ice cream frozen. It had to be carried a bucket at a time up the slippery steps and packed around the ice cream containers. Then the shop floors would be swept. At home he had

First Vallée home (c.1909). Church Street, Westbrook, Maine
(courtesy: Westbrook Historical Society)]

Rudy's childhood home. 36 Monroe Avenue, Westbrook, Maine
(courtesy: Westbrook Historical Society)]

Main Street, Westbrook, Maine (courtesy: Westbrook Historical Society)

Valentine Street Elementary School, Westbrook, Maine
(courtesy: Westbrook Historical Society)

the ashes to clean out of the wood-burning furnace. Only then would he have breakfast and prepare for school. Rudy remembered wryly that when it became his younger brother Bill's turn, the store had coolers and the house a blower furnace! Tough as it was, these early tasks prepared Rudy for the life of a hard worker.

A career as a pharmacist was definitely not what Rudy wanted. His rebelliousness put him constantly at crosses with his father. Charles Vallée was a friendly, gregarious person who genuinely liked people and was interested in their lives. With friends and strangers alike he was congenial, full of stories and good humor. Perhaps the only thing he enjoyed more than visiting was gardening. His vegetable garden was a source of great pride and letters to friends would contain information on the size of his tomatoes and the sweetness of his corn. He took great pride in the fact that he also canned and preserved his own produce. His son showed no interest whatsoever in any of these endeavors and, even at a young age, Rudy could not have ever been considered a "people person."

Despite the affection they both surely felt, Rudy and his father still managed to constantly irritate each other. Both were stubborn but otherwise totally different in interests. In after years, when Rudy was famous and his father so proud of him, they became very close. Still, it was difficult for Rudy to see this friendly dad as the same person who took him on many a trip to the attic to whip with a strap. In Charles' defense it must be acknowledged that Rudy was a headstrong youngster with a quick temper — probably not always easy to live with. Rudy himself admitted that as a boy he had been terrifically passionate with "a lot of feeling and a lot of temper."

One incident particularly escalated out of control. After a quarrel Rudy threatened to run away and join the Navy. Dad Vallée angrily replied that he need not run away as he would personally take him to the recruiting office. The next morning they were both too stubborn to back down. As a result, Rudy soon found himself at the Newport, Rhode

Island Naval Training Station. Later, Charles Vallée would deny he had given false age information to the recruiter. Perhaps not, but he certainly didn't deny it when Rudy signed on. Rudy had completed basic training when the Navy discovered the true age of their fifteen-year-old seaman. He was honorably discharged and sent home. One might guess the Navy didn't discover the truth on their own. There is no doubt that Rudy's mother was not happy about the whole affair.

It may very well be that Charles thought the military experience would do his son some good. Perhaps it might even knock some of the stubbornness out of him. If this was the case, he would be sorely disappointed.

A full-fledged sailor at 15
(courtesy: Westbrook Historical Society)

Katherine Lynch Vallée was a woman of seemingly placid temper. A lover of music and theatricals, she and her oldest son had a warm and understanding relationship. When Rudy was born, Charles decided immediately that his son was destined to be a priest. This was strongly vetoed by Katherine. Later, when Charles determined on a pharmaceutical career for Rudy, she insisted his future lie in the entertainment field, especially music.

During an interview in 1930, Katherine recounted how the young Rudy would sing at little gatherings in their hometown, adding, "He always had that magnetic quality in his voice." At this point Dad Vallée broke in with, "Yes, yes, I always thought he would make a success of his music." An astonished Katherine interrupted him, "Don't you go telling anything of the sort. You know perfectly well you wanted him to be a druggist and take over the store instead of going ahead with his music. If it hadn't been for me, that's what might have become of him." A chastened Charles meekly admitted, "Well perhaps so." Then, with returned spirit, "but I never thought he'd make a good druggist. You can't deny that." She didn't deny that.

Rudy's first book, *Vagabond Dreams Come True* (1930), was dedicated to his mother. Before publication, he diplomatically added: "And

Westbrook High School (courtesy: Westbrook Historical Society)

"The Blue and
White" Yearbook
photo June 1920

THE SCHOOL PLAY

As THE BLUE AND WHITE goes to press, rehearsals are going on for the school play, "A Strenuous Life", a lively, entertaining three-act comedy. Miss Marion Lord of the faculty is acting as coach, and the play will undoubtedly be as great a success as the many previous plays given by the Assembly. The cast is as follows:

Tom Harrington	Hubert Vallée
Reginald Black	Wayland Hendrickson
James Roberts	Harry Corbett
Byron Harrington	Fred Rose
Dan Davenant	Henry McCullough
Professor James	Lenard Jordan
Professor Magee	Harold Fernald
Dawley	Raymond Waite
Marion Davenant	Lillian Welch
Mrs. Wiggins	Alma Townsend
Dulcie Harrington	Grace Burnell
Ruth Thornton	Sally Pickard
Widow Maguire	Cora Hay
Chia	Ruth Knowlton

Business Manager, Harold Fernald.
Assistant Business Manager, Phyllis Sawyer.
Mistress of Properties, Mable Crooker.
Mistress of Wardrobe, Phyllis Cannell.

Senior play starring Hubert Vallée

the mothers of the seven boys who work with me. Were it not for their faith in us, and their great love, we would never have succeeded." It was obviously his bow of appreciation to Katherine.

Back in high school after his Navy hitch, Rudy played saxophone in the school band and had the lead in the senior play. Though admired, he still didn't seem to have any really close friends. There was an aloofness that he projected. Perhaps his Navy experience had given him a maturity to which his classmates couldn't relate. For his yearbook, amongst casually dressed fellow graduates, a nattily dressed Hubert Prior Vallée posed in suit and vest. Young Vallée was described by his contemporaries as one who always wanted to run things, and his general appearance was considered flashy. Acting was his favorite pastime, but fellow students considered him too "jazzy."

1920 high school graduate (courtesy: Westbrook Historical Society)

Theater where Rudy started his career

Reception for a hometown hero

Rudy with father and mother

During his high school years and after yet another quarrel with his father, Rudy again left home, this time only to stay with an acquaintance. Only his mother's tearful pleas brought him home again. He vowed, however, never to work in the drugstore again, and found a job in the local movie house doing janitorial work. When the projectionist didn't come in one night, Rudy got to run the machine. He was in heaven. Working at the theatre was a love second only to playing his beloved saxophone. When he got to play solo on the theatre stage he was hooked for good.

Rudy graduated from high school in 1920 and entered the University of Maine. It was at this time that Hubert acquired the name of "Rudy." He was such a devoted admirer of the saxophonist Rudy Wiedoeft that

Postcard commemorating hometown reception, Vallée Pharmacy in background

fellow students dubbed him with the name that would be his forever. The only time in later life that he used his given name was during service in World War II.

It was at the University that Rudy made what he called his first real buddy. His friend planned to transfer to Yale and convinced Rudy to do the same. The friend eventually changed his mind but Rudy, finding his current romantic interest cooling (she informed him he spent too much time with music and not enough with her), decided to go ahead with the plans to transfer. Rudy was certainly always proud of his Yale degree but held a deep affection for Maine. "Maine Song" is remembered as one of his greatest hits. There is a Rudy Vallée wing at the museum of the University of Maine and he was always most generous in his loyalty.

University of Maine awards "M" to Rudy for making "Stein Song" world famous

Vallée family photo, with brother Bill but missing sister Kathleen c.1930

London Days

To earn enough to pay tuition at Yale, Rudy played saxophone with various local bands. The schedule he kept was grueling. Coming back on campus in the early morning hours, he would have several hours rest before beginning classes. A few hours rest in the afternoon, then some studying, and off again to play at yet another party or dance.

The musical director of the six bands under the management of London's Savoy Hotel heard of Rudy through some Boston musicians then playing in London. On the strength of their recommendations the director offered Rudy $150 a week to come to London and play with the Havana Band. They even suggested he might want to complete his education at London University.

Since he had only been playing the saxophone professionally for one year, Rudy couldn't help but be enormously flattered at the offer. The Savoy was more than just a hotel; it was, as he realized, an institution. Rudy was very much tempted but finally decided to decline. Two years later he was again approached by the Savoy with another offer. By then he was beginning to tire of the strenuous routine of constant playing and studying.

After much thought, Rudy finally decided to accept the Savoy's offer and go to London. It was his plan to spend one year with the Havana Band, save as much of his salary as he could and return to New Haven. It

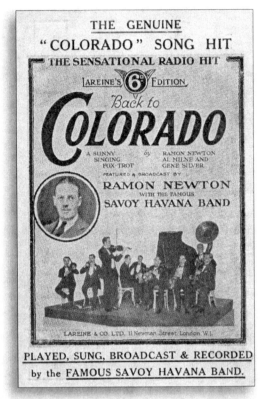

Ad for song hit "Colorado" as played by London's famed Savoy Havana Band

was pleasant to think he could spend his remaining Yale days attending extra lectures and being able, as he thought, "to chum around with some of my classmates." He would then need only to accept enough dance engagements to meet extra expenses.

Rudy sailed for England in the fall of 1924. He was to fill the first saxophone chair with the Savoy Havana Band which comprised eight other men, all English.

The band played for dancing in the evening and at tea time every other afternoon. Living in London was thrilling for the young musician,

Rudy and his ever-ready camera. As a child he turned the family bathroom into a darkroom, developing his own photos

though he was often lonely. Still, he did create some notice. As one writer would comment later, he brought "sex to the sax."

Rudy had the good fortune and privilege to accompany both Beatrice Lillie and Gertrude Lawrence on each of their first records. After one such recording session at the Victor plant some twenty-six miles from London, Rudy needed to get back quickly to the Savoy. Looking around for a musician to give him a lift, he was thrilled when Lillie offered him a ride. The car was filled with recording executives and friends and Rudy happily found himself up by the chauffeur holding a huge armful of flow-

London's famed Savoy

ers. Years later in New York, Rudy and Lillie would be living in the same apartment building. By then, Rudy was the love idol of a million women; and, when interviewed, Beatrice could only sigh, "Oh, yes, we live in the same building but nothing ever happens!"

To augment his income, Rudy gave private saxophone lessons. Unfortunately, he kept his savings in the bottom of his trunk. Returning to his room one day, he found it had been burglarized. His money was gone along with a collection of mementoes of his English stay.

Nevertheless, Rudy decided to stick with his original plan. At the end of the year he announced his intention to return home to college. The Savoy was not happy to lose him and offered him a plum job if he would

To earn extra money while in London, Rudy offered saxophone lessons.
This advertisement he bought and circulated

stay. The Prince of Wales (the future Edward VIII) was interested in learning to play the saxophone, and the job of teaching him was offered to Rudy. It was tempting, but he knew if he kept putting off returning to college he might never go back.

Thirteen years later, he would return to London for the coronation of Edward VIII. This time Rudy was an honored guest at the Savoy. The once-lonely saxophonist was kept busy with theatre and club appearances.

Rudy and his prized Selmer

He was guest of honor at grand receptions and a tea was planned for him to meet the British press — all quite gratifying.

The plan to have a more relaxed college year never happened. Not only did Rudy need the money, but he also now had a reputation. This resulted in more offers to fill with bands than he could possibly accept. Rudy also managed to play with the Yale band and during this time was beginning to form a group that would become known as the Yale Collegians.

A less bright man would have failed academically with such a hectic schedule, but Rudy

As bandleader at the Yale Bowl. This was as close as Rudy got to any real recreation

managed above-average grades and graduated with the class of 1927. At the age of twenty-six he was older than the average graduate and considerably more experienced. His was not a typical college life. Working

Rudy Wiedoeft, his famous pupil
and dancer Alice Weaver

professionally put a distance between him and fellow students, preventing close friendships from developing at college. This was a pattern that would mark his entire career. Rudy would give the appearance of feeling superior to co-workers, arousing an antagonism that would leave him genuinely mystified.

The Vallée Menace

John Held, Jr. would love to have sketched Rudy that first fall out of college. Clad in raccoon coat and wide pants and toting saxophone, record player, records and stand, Rudy made his way to booking offices. A few engagements came along but, as luck would have it, nothing permanent.

After graduating from Yale, Rudy had pulled together a small group of New Haven musicians to form what he called The Yale Collegians. During that summer of 1927 they toured the northeast playing mainly at private clubs and for private parties. Still, Rudy had in his mind playing his saxophone with a big band, not leading one himself.

Early in 1928, a chance conversation with musician-entrepreneur Bert Lown resulted in a job that would change Rudy's life and ultimately the history of radio. A new club was being opened on 53rd Street. The Heigh-Ho Club was small. The owner, Don Dickerman, wanted to attract a society crowd and desired an exclusive and intimate establishment. Since the bandstand was small, the 8-piece Yale Collegians was perfect. The result was a different sound from the big bands that dancers were becoming used to. Opening night was January 8, 1928.

Dickerman was pleased with the band but not with the member doing the singing, and asked Rudy to sing. There were no microphones. Not

Rudy and his megaphone –used before microphones, it became a Vallée symbol

having a powerful voice, Rudy fashioned a megaphone to help him project. Though he used the megaphone only a short time, it became associ-
ated with him. Even today, anyone doing a Rudy Vallée imitation will cup
their hands megaphone fashion.

One night several Yale alumni came into the Heigh-Ho, took one
look at the Collegians and complained. Seems they didn't think the musi-

Rudy and the Connecticut Yankees
Seven original members:
1. Cliff Burwell, pianist & arranger, first violin
2. Manny Lowy, first violin
3. Jules De Vorson, violin
4. Charles Peterson, banjo
5. Joe Miller, saxophone & clarinet
6. Harry Patent, bass violin
7. Ray Toland, drums & traps
added:
8. Phil Buatto, first violin
9. Sid Toplitz, saxophone
10. Walter Gross, pianist

cians looked like Yale men! Instead of changing musicians, Rudy changed their name, and the famous Connecticut Yankees were born. They drew nightly crowds, playing eight hours a night from seven until three in the morning. This included Saturday, Sunday and holidays. Also, they played for a tea dance each Saturday. All of this for $90 a week!

Lown made arrangements with WABC to broadcast from the club. This Atlantic Broadcasting System was later to become CBS. Working

Rudy's Family Poses With Radio Favorite

Photo by Staff Photographer

Rudy Vallee, surrounded by members of his family after the famous radio crooner had alighted from the Flying Yankee this morning. From left to right the photo shows—Rudy's father, Mr. Charles A. Vallee, Rudy Vallee, Mrs. Charles A. Vallee, his mother, Mrs. Kathleen Vallee Lenneville, his sister, and her husband, Prosper Lenneville.

(courtesy: Westbrook Historical Society)

on a tight budget, Rudy couldn't afford an announcer so he did the announcing, singing and directing. The result can only be described as sensational. Women went mad for this radio crooner.

Not everyone was thrilled with the reaction of the female population. A church prelate denounced crooners as "whiners, crying vapid words to impossible tunes." Asked his opinion, conductor Walter Damrosch suggested all crooners "should be drowned!" Such criticisms had no effect on women who continued to adore Rudy.

Lown approached the management of the 81st Street Keith Theatre

THE ENSEMBLE OF "THE FAMOUS HOLLYWOOD CABARET" RESTAURANT, BROADWAY AT 48TH ST., NEW YORK CITY

and convinced them to book Rudy. They reluctantly agreed to a short engagement. On opening night the streets were packed with fans. Inside, enthusiastic women screamed with every song Rudy sang. He was signed to play all the Keith theatres, including the Palace. Recently, an elderly woman told this author how she and her high-school friends cut classes to attend Rudy's performances in Brooklyn. Did they get in trouble? "Oh yes," she said, "but it was all worth it." Even though it happened over seventy years ago, she smiled fondly at the memories. Rudy's mail numbered in the hundreds each day; combined with an unknown number of homemade pies, cakes and candies.

Western Union Telegram had the unfortunate reputation as the bearer of bad news. Their public relations director, George Oslin, hoped to change that by encouraging the public to send "happy" telegrams. At the same time, a Vallée fan in California was sending Rudy a happy birthday telegram. Oslin instructed the New York operator Lucille Lipps to sing the greeting to Rudy over the phone. Thus, on July 23, 1933, he became the recipient of the first singing telegram.

Rudy Vallee Donates Cup For Miss Westbrook Of 1930

DECEMBER 21, 1930

By Staff Photographer

Mrs. Kathleen Vallee Lenneville, a sister of the famous Rudy, and cup which will be presented to Miss Westbrook.

(courtesy: Westbrook Historical Society)

Once asked about his early success, Rudy admitted his limitations but added, "When I said 'love' I meant it and even though it was nasal and thin, the passion was there." That very passion seemed to come through the airwaves. Even Rudy's delivery was different for the day. It was the jazz age. Singers tended to move vigorously with waving hands and swinging

**Rudy's Christmas greeting c.1935. He luckily saw some
humor in the exaggerated stories about his fisticuffs**

bodies. Rudy did none of that. Standing perfectly still at the microphone with eyes half closed, he crooned directly to the listener. The only movement was the occasional caressing of the microphone. Women listeners felt Rudy was singing directly to them. Indeed, he was sued by women who claimed he had wooed them over the air. The idea was ludicrous, but understandable. Later, commenting on his style, Rudy said he closed his eyes to better remember the lyrics!

Charles Laughton told Rudy that he and his wife Elsa Lanchester had caught one of his shows and they had become great fans. Laughton said they both liked the fact that Rudy didn't use the usual artifices which singers employ to hold audiences' attention. He added they liked being able to understand every word. Rudy was especially careful and proud of his diction, so he considered this the finest compliment he had ever received from "anyone whose opinion was really worth anything."

Leonie Cauchois

The debs of the "400" adored Rudy, and the clubs he played were packed every night with women who hoped to catch his eye. Many did get his attention and his love affairs were numerous. But, as Rudy himself admitted, "I have been rather fickle all my life."

One beautiful young woman was special and he fell in love at first sight. Leonie Cauchois was the type he most favored. The dark-eyed brunette was recently divorced and the mother of a young daughter. Within a few weeks she and Rudy were married, but the marriage unfortunately ended just as quickly. Both realized they had been hasty. But as a friend would comment, "This did not cure Rudy. He continued to fall in and out of love with the rising and setting of the sun." The fact was and remained, Rudy genuinely liked women. As he readily admitted, he always needed female companionship.

A humorous article in *Cinema Magazine*, titled "For Husbands Only," purported to advise said husbands how to deal with what was called the "Rudy Vallée menace." The author complained how "this latest home-disrupter sneaks right into your wife's boudoir by crooning to her seductively over the radio while you, innocent soul, are making a speech at the Kiwanis proposing the local radio dealer for membership."

Columnists, of course, had a field day poking fun at the young singer. "Saxophony" and "microphony" and similarly unflattering names were bandied about. One such columnist was Jerry Wald, then a writer for the *New York Graphic*. Every time he made sport of Rudy he received thousands of letters of protest. His publisher, of course, not knowing

Everything Rudy did made headlines, even when he was the target of grapefruit.

the content of the letters, thought it only Wald's fan mail. When Rudy and the Yankees played in Boston and Rudy sang, "Oh, give me something to remember you by," a Harvard student threw a grapefruit at him and missed. Amused by this, Wald suggested a fund to teach Harvard students to throw better! Rudy was not amused.

Later, Wald was called to Hollywood to write for Warner Brothers. One of his first scripts to work on was *Sweet Music* starring Rudy. A warm friendship developed and Wald became a regular guest at Rudy's Maine camp. Wald

Several young women sued Rudy for breach of promise, claiming he wooed them over the air. Frances Singer asked for $250,000. She lost her case!

claimed that Rudy saved his life once when the canoe he was using capsized. Modestly, Rudy suggested that he had to do it else people would think he let him drown on purpose! A more relaxed Vallée was developing a sense of humor.

Rudy denied ever hitting anyone, despite what he called "false historians." It is true that the number of fights were exaggerated by the press. However, there were witnesses to several such occurrences.

Knowing his quick temper, Rudy would steel himself against the usual hecklers. Occasionally, it would become too much of a distrac-

Rudy leaving a theatre with Evelyn Johnson. A photographer
claimed he was hit but Rudy said it was only a push.
Problem? Her husband thought she was in Miami.

Rudy and the Yankees on the Brooklyn Paramount stage.

Rudy kept a hectic schedule in 1929, playing both
the Palace and the Brooklyn Paramount.

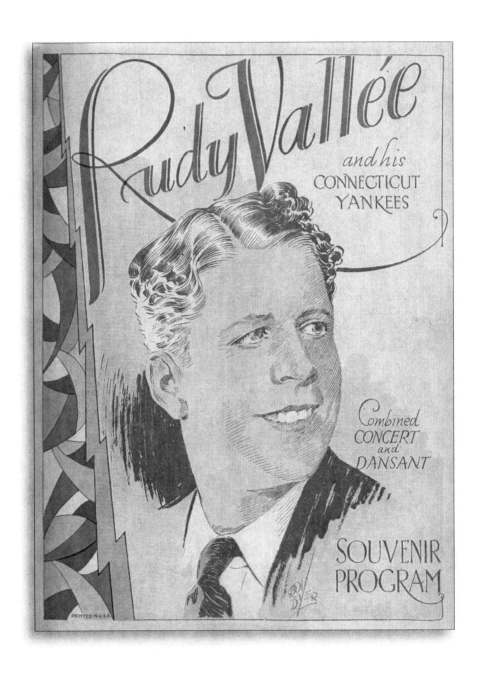

tion. Such a time, playing in Wilkes-Barre, Pennsylvania, two young men were especially persistent. At last, an angry Rudy threw down his baton and charged into the audience. Only quick action by police prevented a brawl. Another time he took on a particularly obnoxious drunk. It was reported the drunk needed assistance to leave.

Another incident happened in Atlantic City while Rudy and the Yankees were playing the Steel Pier ballroom. Near the end of the dance a man began throwing pennies on the stage. Rudy shook his head indicating for him to quit. The culprit only replied, "They're not for you. They're for the dancer. I don't like him." Rudy said he didn't care who they were for and warned the man to desist. "Oh yeah, well, here's one for you" was the only reply. With that, Rudy vaulted to the floor five feet below the level of the stage. He went for the heckler and landed a punch on his jaw. The audience applauded.

From being the target of male wiseacres to one of the most respected men in show business required persistence, sincerity and hard work. Along the way, his own innate sense of humor helped.

When Rudy and the Connecticut Yankees left the Heigh-Ho Club, they moved into the Club Versailles. This club had been doing poorly but soon was packed nightly with Vallée fans. In fact, the owner soon changed the name of the club to Club Vallée. It was meant to be a compliment, but the young singer would have preferred a raise in salary. (This was the same club that would be renamed and become the famous Copacabana.)

It was at this time in late 1929 that Rudy made his first movie appearance. This was in a two-reeler filmed in New York City titled *Campus Sweethearts*. At nine o'clock in the morning he was given a song, "Under a Campus Moon," and told the scene would be shot in one hour. Rudy learned the melody well enough to read the lyrics from a blackboard. The twenty-minute film may possibly be lost.

Rudy signed with NBC that same year - and oh, the power of radio!

Photograph inscribed to Winifred Thompson, President
of Rudy's first fan club (Courtesy: John Wilkes)

Sponsored by Standard Brands, his *Fleischmann Hour* debuted on October 24, 1929. Within one year he had become the most recognized and famous entertainer in the east. Now with his program broadcasting coast to coast every Thursday at eight o'clock, Rudy Vallée fans numbered in

THE MOST ENVIED GIRL IN AMERICA

Hollywood, Calif.—Sally Blane, who will play opposite Rudy Vallee in his first screen appearance in "The Vagabond Lover", helps make-up the possessor of the "voice that thrills" millions of American women, for his movie debut.

Publicity for *The Vagabond Lover* was massive. The studio's expectation that it was "destined to enthrall the world" was sadly delusional

Fay

R udy's entrance into Hollywood in 1928 was nothing short of spectacular, even for a town known for its excesses. Met by a bevy of
beautiful starlets and hundreds of fans, Rudy's entourage (including his
parents) entered Hollywood with a sirened police escort. Rudy's greatest
joy was seeing the pride on his mother's face. All his hard work seemed
worthwhile for that pleasure alone.

His movie, *The Vagabond Lover,* was introduced in one of the biggest publicity blitzes of all times. To say the result was less than satisfying
would be an understate-
ment.

Director Marshall
Neilan was nearing the
end of what had been
a brilliant career and
was drinking heavily.
He took an instant dis-
like to Rudy and to
make matters worse his
current girlfriend de-
veloped a crush on the

Sweet Music **scene recalls
Rudy's reception in Hollywood**

With The Connecticut Yankees in *Vagabond Lover*

The Vagabond Lover cast

young singer. Added to that was the plain fact that Rudy couldn't act! Neilan was not about to make it easier for him.

Rudy always hated the movie and when shortly afterward a studio fire destroyed some films, he regretted *The Vagabond Lover* hadn't been one of them. Many critics predicted it would end his movie career if not damage his popularity significantly. Oddly enough, Vallée fans today love the movie, bad acting and all. It starred a very young and appealing Rudy. As one fan recently remarked, "All he had to do was stand there and look cute. That he did very well!"

While in Hollywood another event occurred that would change his life more than any films. Rudy became acquainted

Sues Ruddy Vallee for $200,000

Agnes O'Loughlin, Broadway chow girl, above, is suing Rudy Vallee, inset, crooner of radio and stage, for $200,0 00, alleging breach of promise. Agnes previously was engaged to Joe Benjamin, former boxer, but brike that off. And prior to that her name was in the public prints when stories appeared saying Jack Dempsey, ex-heavyweight champion, and Benjamin had a fistic tiff in a New York hotel in her presence.

While in Hollywood Rudy was sued for breach of promise, by showgirl Agnes O'Loughlin. He had given her reason to believe he was serious, but once in California he met someone else who consumed all his affections. Agnes settled out of court for $ 1,000

with (and enamored of) Fay Webb. She was the beautiful daughter of Santa Monica's chief of police. The sultry, dark-eyed brunette was the total personification of his ideal woman.

Despite misgivings by friends (and especially his mother) Rudy and Fay were married on July 6, 1931 in West Orange, New Jersey. They were on their honeymoon when Rudy received word that his mother was seriously ill. As he prepared to hurry to Maine, he was astonished and angry when Fay refused to accompany him. Rudy left alone and was able

Rudy and His Beautiful Bride

They're smiling, sure they are! But how about those flappers all over America—what have they to smile about now? For Rudy Vallee, soft-voiced crooner of love songs, has a wife. And here she is—Fay Webb, former screen actress—as she posed with Rudy in New York for the first time since their secret marriage at West Orange, N. J.

Announcement of the surprise wedding of Rudy Vallée and
Fay Webb brought grief to a multitude of women.

to be with his mother for two days. An iron cot was put in her room where he slept close enough for him to hold her hand. After Katherine died, Fay arrived by train and was met by a heartbroken Rudy. At the funeral Fay fainted. Newspapers reported that she had fainted from grief.

It was the last family funeral Rudy would ever attend. There were townsfolk who thought it strange and unfeeling he did not return, particularly for his father's and

Fay and Rudy 1931

sister Kathleen's services. The religious significance meant little to Rudy and it wasn't the way he wanted to remember those he loved.

Rudy and Fay were married barely two years when it all fell apart. Fay refused to accompany Rudy on the road when he traveled with his band and regularly went back home to California for extended visits. Friends commented that this was odd behavior for a bride. What they didn't know and Fay evidently never talked about was her fragile health. She was very close to her family and there was security there with them that she didn't find in New York. The warm California weather also was more agreeable.

Fay was certainly insecure and desperately jealous of the women with whom Rudy worked, especially Frances Langford. She demanded that he stop working with Frances, and he acceded to her wishes. Alice

Fay in pensive mood while visiting parents in California and with roses from Rudy

Rudy in the comics

Fay sues for divorce

Faye, however, was a different matter and Rudy refused to agree to Fay's demands. To give his wife credit, her suspicions were not without credence. Later, despite his steady stream of love affairs, Alice's was the only photograph Rudy kept by his bedside. So closely connected were they in peoples' minds that even today Alice is listed in many books as one of his wives.

Alice Faye with Rudy 1933

Despite his other interests, Rudy's love for Fay bordered on an obsession. He held a vision in his mind that a wife should fit and she did not. It made him desperately unhappy and finally an event occurred that caused an irreversible split.

Rudy's brother Bill disliked Fay intensely and was convinced she was unfaithful. When Rudy was away and Bill was alone in the apartment he connected the telephone lines to a recording disc. Though this conduct was certainly ethically questionable, it was not at that time illegal. Bill got the information he wanted. While Rudy was away, Fay phoned her alleged lover, dancer Gary Leon. The explicitly sexy conversation was the evidence Bill needed to convince Rudy that he should leave Fay.

More headlines

It is doubtful that Rudy had any idea of the firestorm the separation would cause. The whole matter made front page headlines in even major newspapers. Untold numbers of editorials were written condemning the whole affair. Only a portion of the recorded conversation was released to the public which, of course, set imaginations working overtime. Fay filed for divorce naming Alice Faye as the other woman, plus at least two other "Jane Does."

Rudy agreed to the divorce and offered alimony of one hundred dol-

lars a month. A compromise on money no doubt would have been reached but Fay insisted on nothing less then ninety thousand dollars per year, an enormous sum in those Depression years. It was at this point that Rudy released the entire recorded conversations. Some members of the press originally presented him as ungallant for doing so. He felt forced into it by Fay's exorbitant demands. Rudy was convinced that Fay thought he placed his career above everything in the world and would not risk it by any more bad publicity. As he explained at the time, "I have pride as an individual as well as a celebrity, and I have a sense of justice."

As the case developed, magazines and newspaper editorials sided more with Rudy. Fay was pictured as avaricious and immoral. Fairness requires we acknowledge that Rudy was not always easy to live with. He had a quick temper and certainly a double standard in man-woman relationships. He demanded much of his wife and either was not aware of or was insensitive to Fay's increasing physical weakness. When they married, her weight was near one hundred and twenty pounds. By the time of their separation she weighed barely a hundred pounds.

Director Eddie Sutherland (l) gives instructions on the set of Paramount's
International House. **It was a painful time in Rudy's life**

Despite positive reaction toward him, Rudy was anxious to have the whole business over with. He was beginning to be the subject of jokes. "Let's drop in on Rudy Vallée some evening and listen to records, he has some honeys!" Such humor was embarrassing to someone who prided himself at that time on public dignity.

During the divorce trial, Fay was often absent from the courtroom. Newspapers saw this as a sign of a weak case and scoffed at her lawyers' insistence that she was ill.

After the divorce was final, Rudy quietly gave Fay an additional twenty-five thousand dollars. When news of the gift became public knowledge, rumors began to fly. Since he had said she could have one hundred dollars a week and no more, the questions were raised as to what

Last known photograph of Fay, taken in the garden of her parents' home, 1936

happened. A payment to keep her quiet? A reconciliation perhaps? But Rudy remained silent. The facts were, when Rudy realized how very ill his ex-wife really was, he sent her the additional money for medical expenses. Barely six months after the divorce Fay Webb was dead of tuberculosis.

In his memoirs, Rudy recalled her death in an unusually callous man-

Fay's funeral, November 22, 1936, Santa Monica, California. Wreath from Rudy above casket

ner, saying that Fay had died "between drugs, liquor, incipient TB and three or four beach boys in an afternoon." Why he felt it necessary to write such harsh words we can only guess. Perhaps he chose not to remember how great had been his grief when he heard the news.

On the day Fay died, an unhappy and distraught Rudy hurried to the home of his close friend Adela Rogers St. Johns. He had never let anything keep him from fulfilling commitments. But he felt he could never manage to do his show that week. He needed reassurance and Adela told him, "No one will blame you, Rudy, for staying away." Later, recalling that visit, she said, "I for one am glad that he missed that broadcast. Because of his silence he paid the woman, he had once dearly loved the greatest tribute he could have paid her. On her grave he laid a wreath of silence."

Actually, he laid another wreath. At the head of Fay's coffin was a huge arrangement of gardenias and orchids with heather fringe. They had come from Rudy with a poignant note, "I had never stopped loving her." It would take years for the wounds to heal.

Durium "Hit-of-the-Week" paper record (1931). These single-sided flexible discs sold for 10¢ each, usually on newsstands. Rudy, along with many other singers, made these records until the company closed in 1932

Rudy was kept busy throughout the 1930s

Rudy being toasted by Robert Montgomery and George Raft, NYC nightclub, 1934

On the Air

The Great Depression was being felt even by show business stars. By late 1931, an incredibly hard-working Rudy was joined by only three others who became millionaires since the crash of 1929; the others being Maurice Chevalier and Freeman F. Gosden and Charles J. Correll (Amos 'n Andy).

During those early 1930s Rudy worked at a furious pace, often getting by with four or five hours sleep a night. There were the innumerable club dates, movies, charity appearances and performances on Broadway in *George White's Scandals*. A close friend once confided that Rudy reminded her "a little pitifully, of a squirrel in a cage. As he climbs the cage turns. The higher and faster he climbs, the faster the cage turns. He's at his peak now,

Gathering of stars of various NBC affiliates, including Rudy (3rd from left) and Kate Smith]

Wielding the baton

and he must work furiously to stay there or the cage will spin away under him."

Throughout the 1930s Rudy was also managing to contribute articles to various publications. A natural writer, his features were articulate and often provocative. Literate and honest, his columns delighted readers, but not always other entertainers. One of the best of his series was "It's My Humble Opinion," which ran for

Rudy with NBC orchestra.

January, 1936   LADIES' HOME JOURNAL   49

R*udy* VALLÉE *says . . .*

"PUT YOURSELF ACROSS"

America has lost her heart to him—this charming youth who thrills millions with his crooning voice so full of magnetism, pathos, life. What has he that others envy? Is it merely added energy, added physical "drive"?

"For that subtle 'added ounce' of energy I follow the simple advice of great physicians"

"How you feel has a lot to do with how people feel *about* you," says Rudy Vallée.

"Lots of folks handicap themselves by getting run-down—sluggish and out of order physically. Naturally they can't 'put themselves across.' They are *half sick*.

"When I was rehearsing for the Fleischmann Radio Hour I heard so much about yeast that I decided to try it. I was under a terrific strain —playing, singing, rehearsing, planning my talking, singing picture, 'The Vagabond Lover.'

Well, what the famous physicians say about yeast certainly worked out in my case. It gave me just that 'added ounce' of energy I needed to keep fresh and 'on my toes.'"

A remarkable *food*, Fleischmann's Yeast brings you quick new energy by purifying and stimulating your whole digestive tract. Elimination becomes regular, *complete*. Appetite and digestion improve. Complexion troubles disappear.

Start today! You can get Fleischmann's Yeast at grocers, restaurants, soda fountains.

EAT THREE CAKES *of Fleischmann's fresh Yeast daily, one before each meal or between meals, just plain or dissolved in water. Every cake now contains two vitamins indispensable to health—vitamin B and the "sunshine" vitamin D.*

Rudy's face was selling everything from yeast cakes to jukeboxes

They gave a *new* Thrill

THAT'S WHY THEY GOT THERE....SO QUICKLY

"*So you're a saxophone player, eh? Well . . . make me weep! Do your stuff,*" said the vaudeville booker. Rudy did! And fame caressed him. The whole public succumbed in two short years.

RUDY VALLÉE

Two years ago he stepped into the spot-light on a little cafe floor and crooned a song called "Deep Night." Today deep night on Broadway sees his name blazed in electric signs.

. . .

It wasn't the cut of his clothes . . . or the break of his luck. This youngster just naturally delivered something that the public wants!

Just so OLD GOLD cigarettes have grown from a baby brand to a giant brand in record time . . . because they delivered a new enjoyment . . . they thrilled the taste and comforted the most sensitive throat.

Better tobaccos...that's why they win.

On March 7, 1927, OLD GOLDS were introduced in Illinois. Today, the city of Chicago alone smokes nearly 3,000,000 daily.

© P. Lorillard Co.

BETTER TOBACCOS . . . "NOT A COUGH IN A CARLOAD"

And it's "Sweet Music" for Rudy Vallee, his first picture under Warner Brothers' tutelage. He'll be making more of the same for this company which is famous for its musicals. Rudy's pretty much in demand between radio and screen. People still ask about Alice.

several years in *Radio Stars* magazine. The title was certainly misleading as it definitely was not humble, but was very Vallée. Here Rudy had the opportunity to give his opinion on a wide range of subjects, something he always loved doing. There were those who viewed him as an intellectual snob. This always puzzled Rudy, as he was, after all, only giving his honest opinion on a vast number of topics. One of his chief dislikes was Hollywood premieres. He called them an "orgy of showoffs and show-

With Helen Morgan in *Sweet Music*

ing off" and "the most sickening of the entire proceedings are the stupid microphonic mouthings and dolorous dribble that emanate from the mouths of the glamorous film stars themselves." There were, no doubt, many who agreed with him; but would understand that this wasn't a tactful opinion to express, not if you wanted to win friends and influence the powers in filmdom. But this didn't worry Rudy. He was still riding a crest of popularity as one of America's most famous men.

In 1934, Rudy starred in *Sweet Music*, a movie that totally captured his true personality. His character was a singer-bandleader with legions of adoring female fans. Rudy exuded charm, and while still not a polished actor, his vanity, humor and romance came through on screen. No doubt much of that semi-biographical portrayal is the reason *Sweet Music* has

Sweet Music cast: Al Shean, Alice White, Allen Jenkins, Rudy Vallée, Ned Sparks, Ann Dvorak, Joseph Cawthorn]

remained the all-time favorite with Vallée fans. To add extra interest at the time, two versions of the title song were written by Al Dubin and Harry Warren and introduced on Rudy's radio show. Fans could vote for the one they liked better. The winning song was used in the film.

Throughout this period his radio show would be number one, with listeners numbering in the millions. *The Fleischmann Hour* set the standard for every variety show that would come after. Airing Thursday evenings over NBC, it was the first real variety talk show and guests were interviewed in addition to performing. There were skits, serious and humorous, featuring the famous and soon-to-be famous. No other person has ever introduced such a vast array of talent to the American public.

Critics have questioned Rudy's role in choosing talent. Certainly at

A caricature of Rudy seemed to appear everywhere – even on Valentines

times, personalities were brought to his attention by others, but it was Rudy who had the final word. It was Rudy's personality that brought out their talent and his popularity which made it all possible.

For ten years he reigned supreme on the air. Eddie Cantor had his radio debut on the *Fleischmann Hour*, as did Burns and Allen, Kate Smith and Bob Hope. Gene Autry's fledgling career thrived after his appearance. Others who could directly attribute their success to Rudy include Edgar Bergen, Alice Faye, Frances Langford, Dorothy Lamour and Red Skelton.

An appearance on the *Fleischmann Hour* practically guaranteed success for a talented performer. During the 1930s radio editors would select the outstanding new star of the year. The award in 1933 (the first) went to Joe Penner. In 1934 Helen Jepson was named; Bob Burns got the award in 1935, and in 1936 the winner was Frank Fay. All had made their

T   V A L L E E

H

E   V O I C E

APRIL
'39

R esourceful
U nselfish
D evoted
Y outhful

V ersatile
A lert
L ikeable
L oyal
E arnest
E nthusiastic

Fan clubs flourished from coast to coast. Rudy not only encouraged and supported them with letters and photos, but both his father and brother Bill contributed stories. These covers had snapshots: Rudy with his ever-present camera and his Waring blender (a gift from inventor Fred Waring)

Still reaping the rewards of advertising

first radio appearance with Rudy. The material awards were, of course, enormous. Bergen had been performing at the Los Angeles Paramount for $300 a week. After appearing on Rudy's show, his salary jumped to $10,000 a week! Red Skelton moved from being a $ 400 a week player to signing for $2,000 a week at RKO.

No one has been recorded as having turned down a chance to be on Rudy's show. Dr. Allan Dafoe, of Dionne Quintuplets fame, had refused to appear on any commercial radio show until Rudy convinced him to come on his program. The experience was so pleasant, the doctor agreed to his own three-a-week series.

Though Rudy often expressed an aversion to children, Rose Marie appeared several times on his show. She remembers him as being very sweet

SOME NEW ICE CREAM RECIPES CREATED BY THE SEALTEST KITCHEN

Vallée puzzles to solve ... and put together

and incredibly kind and helpful. Years later, finding some rare photos of the two of them, Rudy presented them to her as a remembrance.

Entertainers of color had a difficult time finding spots on radio shows. Rudy was the only star who regularly had them on. Maxine Sullivan, Josephine Baker, Bill Robinson, Carmen MacRae, Stepin Fetchit, Ford L. Washington and John Sublett (Buck & Bubbles), and Eddie Green were but a few who were welcomed on the Vallée show. Even ever-modest heavy-weight champ Joe Louis agreed to appear for an interview. When Rudy took his vacation in 1936, he insisted his sponsor hire Louis Armstrong as his substitute — the first time an African-American performer would host

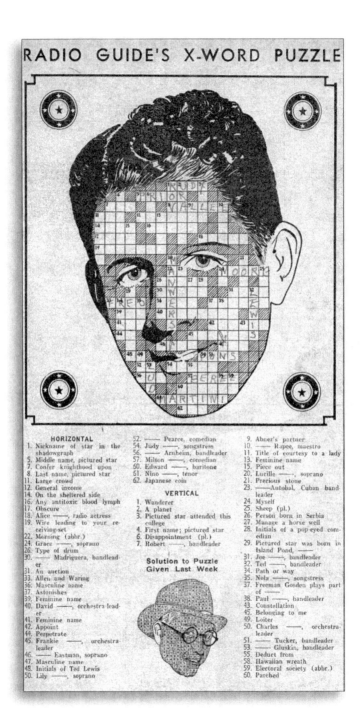

RADIO GUIDE'S X-WORD PUZZLE

HORIZONTAL

1. Nickname of star in the shadowgraph
5. Middle name, pictured star
7. Confer knighthood upon
8. Last name, pictured star
11. Large crowd
12. General income
14. On the sheltered side
16. Any antitoxic blood lymph
17. Obscure
18. Alice ———, radio actress
19. Wire leading to your receiving-set
22. Morning (abbr.)
24. Grace ———, soprano
26. Type of drum
30. ——— Madriguera, bandleader
31. An auction
33. Allen and Waring
36. Masculine name
37. Astonishes
39. Feminine name
40. David ———, orchestra leader
41. Feminine name
42. Appoint
44. Perpetrate
45. Frankie ———, orchestra leader
46. ——— Eastman, soprano
47. Masculine name
48. Initials of Ted Lewis
50. Lily ———, soprano

52. ——— Pearce, comedian
54. Judy ———, songstress
56. ——— Arnheim, bandleader
57. Milton ———, comedian
60. Edward ———, baritone
61. Nino ———, tenor
62. Japanese coin

VERTICAL

1. Wanderer
2. A planet
3. Pictured star attended this college
4. First name; pictured star
6. Disappointment (pl.)
7. Robert ———, bandleader

**Solution to Puzzle
Given Last Week**

9. Abner's partner
10. ——— Rapee, maestro
11. Title of courtesy to a lady
13. Feminine name
15. Piece out
20. Lucille ———, soprano
21. Precious stone
23. ———Autobal, Cuban bandleader
24. Myself
25. Sheep (pl.)
26. Person born in Serbia
27. Manage a horse well
28. Initials of a pop-eyed comedian
29. Pictured star was born in Island Pond, ———
31. Joe ———, bandleader
32. Ted ———, bandleader
34. Path or way
35. Nola ———, songstress
37. Freeman Gosden plays part of ———
38. Paul ———, bandleader
43. Constellation
45. Belonging to me
49. Loiter
50. Charles ———, orchestra leader
51. ——— Tucker, bandleader
53. ——— Gluskin, bandleader
55. Deduct from
58. Hawaiian wreath
59. Electoral society (abbr.)
60. Parched

Off to the 1933 Chicago World's Fair with Alice Faye and unidentified troupe

a national radio program. Rudy greatly admired honest talent wherever found; whatever faults he might have had, bigotry was not one of them.

Some of the *Fleischmann Hour* shows originated from clubs. It was an excellent way to combine club appearances with his radio variety programs. The remote broadcasts from the Astor Roof in New York City were especially popular with audiences. So enthusiastic were female fans that Rudy was brought in, for his own protection, in what was actually described as a glass cage.

For an unprecedented ten years, Rudy would be sponsored by Standard Brands, makers of Fleischmann's Yeast and Royal Gelatin. The latter was advertised for his last three years. It is astonishing how little credit Rudy has received for his extraordinary contribution to the history of radio. As time went on, and its history was being written, Rudy became increasingly bitter about the oversight and rightly so.

In 1931 Rudy made his stage debut in a musical, *George White's Scan-*

Headliner at the Pan-American Exposition, Dallas, Texas, 1937

dals. The show was an instant success, with Rudy introducing the famed "Life is Just a Bowl of Cherries." Not so harmonious was Vallée's relationship with White. In 1934, when White planned his *Scandals* movie, he wanted Rudy for the lead. He appealed to Vallée to let bygones be bygones. Rudy finally agreed but only on the condition that Alice Faye be given a part in the film. White balked at this; Alice had never made a movie and was known as just a girl singer. But he wanted Rudy and to get him, he agreed to Alice. It was a decision he never regretted. When Alice Faye became a superstar, White could claim he introduced her. For Rudy, starring with Alice was the only pleasant part of the experience. His relationship with White never improved with age.

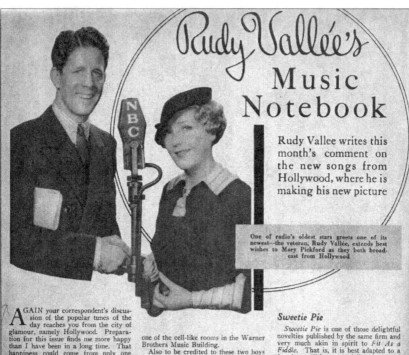

Rudy Vallée's
Music
Notebook

Rudy Vallee writes this month's comment on the new songs from Hollywood, where he is making his new picture

One of radio's oldest stars greets one of its newest—the veteran, Rudy Vallée, extends best wishes to Mary Pickford as they both broadcast from Hollywood

AGAIN your correspondent's discussion of the popular tunes of the day reaches you from the city of glamour, namely Hollywood. Preparation for this issue finds me more happy than I have been in a long time. That happiness could come from only one thing—that is the feeling that I am in the hands of the film company which has made and is making the finest musical pictures, and I am extremely fortunate in having as my boss, Hal Wallis, one of the finest, keenest and most likeable men I have ever met, and having as a director Al Green, whose twenty years of picture experience have endeared him to everyone who knows him. I have often felt that good things come in threes, and I feel that this dip into pictures is going as I said in a recent Thursday broadcast to be a very happy one for me.

Happiness Ahead

Thursday's feeling might well be crystallized into the title of a Warner Brothers' picture, *Happiness Ahead,* that boasts of three excellent songs.

The first song, *Happiness Ahead,* is introduced in a novel fashion. Before the actual title of the picture, Dick Powell appears and sings a chorus of the song, then the actual first sequence flashes on the screen. This particular composition was written by my old friend Allie Wrubel, the Wesleyan College saxophonist, who is now one of the "fair-haired" boys on the Warner lot. Together with Mort Dixon, Allie has

one of the cell-like rooms in the Warner Brothers Music Building.

Also to be credited to these two boys is *Pop Goes Your Heart,* which is unquestionably the best song from the picture. It is a rhythmical type of composition, with the "pop" occurring at the top of an ascending musical figure.

Beauty Must Be Loved

The third song, *Beauty Must Be Loved,* is from the pens of Sammy Fain and Irving Kahal. These two boys are evidently going to be responsible for about eighty per cent of the songs which will appear in my picture. Sammy Fain is an excellent singer himself, and an excellent accompanist at the piano. Therefore it is not to be wondered at that he is beginning to turn out some of the best songs that have appeared in the Warner Brothers pictures. This one, however, in my opinion is the exception that proves the rule, being just a fair song. It is spotted in a sequence which finds Dick and his young, happy, but poor friends in an apartment while he sings it to them at the piano. The picture is an excellent one, and the score well adapted to its presentation in the film. But I believe that, with the exception of *Pop Goes Your Heart* it will not be calculated to achieve any unusual fame for its composers.

Sweetie Pie

Sweetie Pie is one of those delightful novelties published by the same firm and very much akin in spirit to *Fit As a Fiddle.* That is, it is best adapted to a female rendition, especially by a girl trio or a very young lady, let us say on the type of Mitzi Green, a song that deserves more than passing mention and one which should be played quite brightly.

Autumn Night

In The Quiet Of An Autumn Night was written by two young talented friends of mine—Pat Ballard and Charlie Henderson. Charlie, my pianist at my Lombardy Hotel engagement in 1928, when together we wrote *Deep Night,* has since been one of the pillars of the Waring aggregation, but now has aspirations to producing music especially for radio, rehearsing acts for radio consumption, and occasionally turning out a popular hit. *In The Quiet Of An Autumn Night* is one of the most played songs on the air, and the very least I can do is call it to your attention. It is published by DeSylva, Brown and Henderson, and should be played quite slowly.

Rain

Rain is a clear cut example of a publisher's attempt to have its staff writers put into songs [Continued on page 49]

22   RADIOLAND

One of Rudy's many magazine articles, interesting for the fact that he says he is in Hollywood to make a movie and never mentions its name (*Sweet Music*), One wonders why . . . he is not usually this modest.

The Private Life of Rudy Vallee

Rudy Vallee, Public Crooner No. 1, has an intense dislike for publicity regarding his private life. Many women have loved the young man from Maine, but do you know how many have married him? Do you know why he first was called Rudy, or where he goes to forget his cares? Have you ever read Rudy's Rules of Etiquette for his guests, and do you know what single action he warns them most against? These and scores of other interesting questions about one of America's most popular young men are answered in the next issue of LOOK. Get a LOOK; you'll like it.

In the Next Issue of

Look

On sale all newsstands, Tuesday, Oct. 26

FILL OUT COUPON NOW

LOOK, Incorporated, Des Moines, Iowa: Enclosed is $2.50*. Please send Look for 1 year (26 issues) to the following address:

NAME_____

STREET_____

TOWN_____

STATE_____
*Canadian $2.50—Foreign $3.50   10-12

Rudy's face appears constantly on magazine covers. Unfortunately his private life is also featured, much to his discomfort.

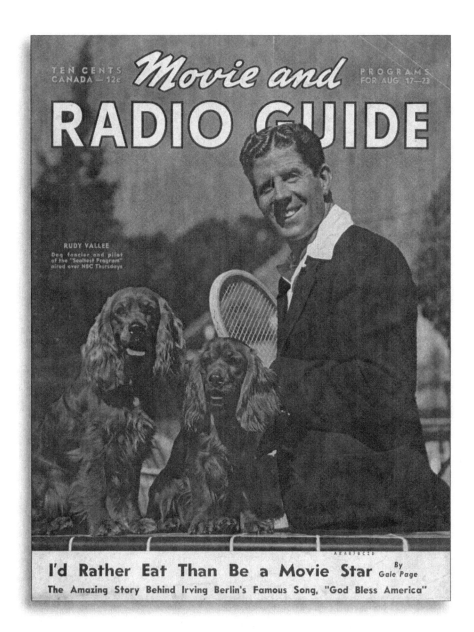

To swing or not to s

stormy question. He

and music for you to d

Maxine Sullivan, left, whose
swing version of the old song
started all the controversy.

Opponents of swing music objected to singers who they believed "ruined"
old songs. Maxine Sullivan's popular upbeat version of "Loch Lomond" was
particularly denounced. Sullivan was a frequent guest on Vallée's shows.

Though hundreds of guests would appear on the Vallée show, none
were more interesting than Helen Keller. Her appearance was inspired by
an incident in Rudy's life. Early in the 1930s Rudy received a letter from
Margaret Young, a young blind girl, who told him how much his singing meant to her. Rudy answered her letter, later learning she was living

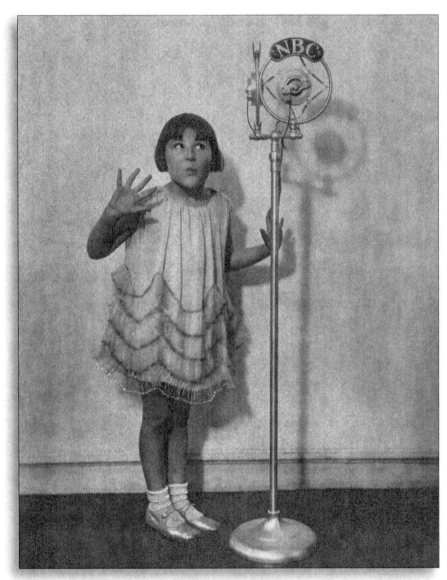

Rose Marie made several appearances with Vallée. She remembers
the times with great pleasure, saying Rudy was very sweet and generous.
Though he didn't generally care for children, Rudy seemed to make
an exception where most professional kids were concerned —
perhaps most exhibited the discipline he admired.

The largest selling ham in the world

The ham that never varies! Always the same! You can be sure of its exquisite tenderness, its mildness, its "hammy" flavor.

The Ham What Am!

This satiric "ad" was to appear in a popular entertainment magazine. When the editor discovered there was a death in Rudy's family he had the face removed, thinking it not the time to razz the singer. It was so obviously meant to be Vallée that faceless it caused more of a stir than otherwise would have happened.

RUDY VALLÉE, EVER IN THE CAMERA'S EYE

(1) Lucky Rose Marie, to be the pupil of our Rudy. Graham McNamee looks on in approval.
(2) The redoubtable "Dazzy" Vance and the heavy slugging "Babe" Herman, of the Brooklyn Dodgers, learn a little about the saxophone from our idol.
(3) Rudy pays a social call to the boys on the Flagship U. S. S. Oklahoma, and meets the mascot.
(4) Max Ello, world's greatest tumbler, lends Rudy support on a difficult "sax" solo.
(5) "The Chinese Rudy Vallée" croons "A Little Kiss Each Morning" to his mentor.
(6) Rudy is made an honorary Lieutenant of Company H, 14th Infantry, New York National Guard.

(From concert program)

in poor circumstances. He insisted on sending her a monthly allowance, continuing to do so as long as she lived. This generous side of Rudy, unfortunately, is not well known.

In 1938 Rudy starred with Rosemary Lane in the musical *Gold Diggers in Paris*. A pleasant movie with choreography by Busby Berkeley, it was mildly successful but failed to match previous *Gold Digger* hits. Tastes were changing and standard 1930s musicals were being considered passé. As it turned out, it would also be the last movie in which Rudy would have the sole romantic lead.

Paradise in the Pines

During the hectic, hardworking and sometimes heartbreaking period of the 1930s, Rudy's salvation was in the Maine woods. Every Thursday from the last of April until the first of November, as soon as his broadcast was finished, he would dash for the express elevator. Avoiding fans and autograph seekers, Rudy rushed to a waiting car. With motorcycle escorts he quickly arrived at Grand Central Station where a train was being held past time especially for him.

Before the train had barely pulled away from New York City, Rudy would begin to relax. For four days he could forget his cares and recoup in his own private paradise.

Rudy enjoyed this time of leisure, even doing his own grocery shopping in town. Occasionally, he would leave the camp for a charity event, but other than that he preferred not to perform. At that time he was doing an average of one hundred charities a year. Later, he found some of them were benefiting the promoters more than the charity. After he led a crusade to keep charities totally honest, many promoters publicly denounced him as a tightwad.

Rudy's three-hundred-acre Lodge was located on the beautiful Lake Kezar, south of the White Mountain National Forest. New visitors were

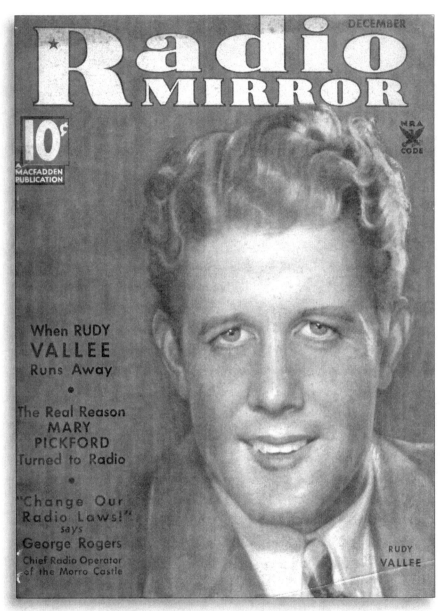

A feature story on Rudy, "When Rudy Vallée Runs Away."
The "away" was a private lodge in Maine.

Entrance to the Vallée Lodge

amazed at the amenities. The first time out they expected to rough it in the woods. Instead, they were treated to elegant quarters. All the rooms in the various buildings were named for songs; Rudy's, of course, being "Vagabond Lover." There were "Betty Co-Ed," "Pink Lady," "Stein Song" and others. Alice Faye's room was "Nasty Man," the title of her first hit song. Each room had a special color scheme to fit the name. The special touches always created a delighted surprise. Cigarette boxes carried out the color scheme of the room and when lifted played the correct song. Everything was perfectly organized and beautifully equipped.

The "Pirates' Den" was playroom and boathouse combined. The pool table was a gift from Frances Langford and the huge bar came from Dorothy Lamour. Other personal gifts were scattered throughout the Lodge, each one engraved with donor's name and date.

The original building, renovated 1936

Pool table and bar on the upper floor of Boathouse decorated
with photos of Rudy and framed sheet music

Dining room fireplace with "My Time is Your Time" carved on mantle

Rudy enjoyed playing the host and there were always guests there to enjoy his hospitality. During the month of July he provided a bus for any of his band members or staff who wanted to come. They were welcome to bring a guest with them, providing a lovely vacation for families.

Rudy had a mania for neatness and orderliness which he said he had inherited from his mother. He couldn't comprehend how anyone could be anything but neat and clean. But he sadly had to admit that there were many who could leave a bathroom in a mess without a thought, and drop cigarette butts on the floor as a matter of habit. Knowing this, Rudy compiled a set of rules for guests. Some folks were annoyed, but most visitors found them amusing; and what's more, they were for the most part heeded.

Each guest received a copy of LODGE LOGIC AND YOUR EC-

CENTRIC HOST, which included such admonitions as:

> Kindly put things back where and as you find them.
>
> Don't over-eat, over-drink, over-exercise. You'll be ill and spoil your enjoyment of Lake Kezar and the Lodge if you do.
>
> DON'T throw large pieces of paper or bulky things into the toilet bowls; they clog easily and plumbers must come 25 miles to undo the damage.
>
> DON'T leave towels on the bathroom floor or in your room—put them in the hampers, that's what hampers are for.
>
> Servants . . . ARE NOT HERE TO: {among seven items} Pick up YOUR cigarette ends, cigar ends, chewing gum paper, cellophane wrappers . . . , etc.

There were over fifty such rules and regulations and suggestions ending with:

> Relax . . . Stretch as the cat does, often and completely . . . Walk and swim plenty . . . Above all don't talk shop.

The booklets were amusingly illustrated by his artistically talented brother Bill. The Rules were not supposed to be removed from the rooms, but somehow they seemed to disappear to become prized souvenirs.

Rudy took to heart his own rule about relaxing. Once at his Lodge, a different man would emerge. The New York taskmaster relaxed in the warmth of the sun. Reserve seemed to fall away and he enjoyed making home movies, swimming and shopping for groceries. Though known for his sartorial elegance, the only time Rudy dressed up at the Lodge was when he took the wheel of his beloved Chris-Craft speed boat. Then, he

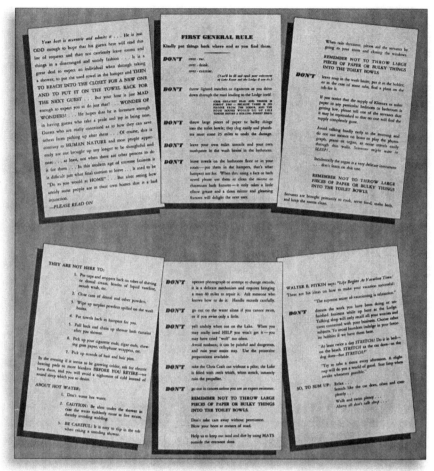

A few of the Rules

often wore his navy whites.

He liked to point out that the boat was a gift from Eddie Cantor. The story behind the gift tells much about Rudy and his fabled frugality.

Some time earlier he had called Guy Lombardo and asked about buying a speed boat. Lombardo's favorite pastime was racing boats so it was thought he could find a good bargain. Shortly Guy called back and gave a

On the lake with "Banjo Eyes"

price. There was silence for a moment before Rudy exclaimed that he had meant "a used one." Guy said he'd look around for one and several weeks later called with the price of an excellent used speed boat. Rudy said he'd think about it and call him back. Guy never got that call.

Later, an ill Cantor needed a substitute for his show and the producer called Rudy. In those days stars were not paid to substitute for another performer. They could ask for a return exchange for their own show or accept a gift. Rudy opted for the gift and requested a new speed boat! Evidently, Eddie took the request in stride and sent the gift. The two men remained close friends, and the boat was christened *Banjo Eyes*. Every day when the weather allowed, fifteen or twenty guests would board the cruiser. Rudy would take it about a mile out where they would anchor

Guy Lombardo aboard his boat *The Tempo*

and enjoy lunch. This ritual was said to be the chief delight of his guests.

On days with inclement weather, there were movies to watch, an excellent library to browse, and always music. Rudy claimed there was a variety of music, but guests would recall a lot of the Vallée voice! For moonlight cruises, Rudy liked Hawaiian music and was especially fond of Dorothy Lamour's "The Moon of Manakoora."

By the late 1940s, finances were becoming tighter and engagements less lucrative. Looking at ways to continue his comfortable lifestyle, Rudy put the Lodge up for sale. In his mem-

Eddie Cantor, the original "Banjo Eyes"

**Swimming with Alice and
unidentified guest (*Look Magazine*,
November 1937)**

Dorothy Lamour, one of Rudy's
proudest discoveries

Rudy with radio cast, c.1937

Skiing in Maine – Note Rudy's proud "M"

**Relaxing with Rose & Hugh Herbert and Jack Dempsey.
Herbert appeared in 1938's *Gold Diggers in Paris***

oirs he passed it off as of no consequence. It had been fun, but that was in the past. It was time to get rid of it, move on and not look back. As with many of Rudy's statements about not caring for the past, it was brave talk. Actually, letting go of the Lodge was heart-wrenching. It was a treasure that had been there when he was sorely in need of mental and physical renewal. Truly, it had been a paradise. Now it was gone and its going saddened him.

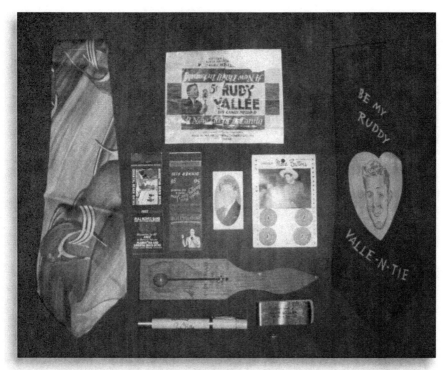

Rudy Vallée souvenirs were collectable and wildly popular with fans

October 25, 1939. Rudy placing his feet and hand prints in cement at the Court of Fame, Schaefer Center, at the New York World's Fair. The Hollywood ceremony would take place on July 21, 1941

RADIO'S PHOTO-MIRROR

Back in New York after filming *Second Fiddle,*
the movie that introduced Sonja Henie to the American public

The Fun Years

Rudy was restless. Ten years is a long time to host a radio show. He was also astute enough to know times were changing and his format was beginning to grow stale. A change of direction was needed, but what? From childhood, music had been his great love. Leading and playing in a band was his one dream. Now, oddly enough, he was weary of it. Rudy decided to disband the Connecticut Yankees. It was a hard decision, but once done he felt strangely liberated.

Roscoe Ates, James Cagney, RV, Phil Regan
(courtesy: Chuck Thompson)

Nice publicity page for starlet Susan Ridgeway,
but not one of Rudy's serious romances

Despite his oft-repeated lack of patience with children, Rudy
poses happily with Jimmy Wallington's two offspring and
columnist Jimmy Fidler (l.), Ken Murray, Wallington (r.)

Now free to pursue other avenues, all sorts of ideas and latent ambitions were considered. A talent agency perhaps — he certainly had the experience finding and promoting talent. The result, Rudy Vallée Presents, Inc., was a great idea, but Rudy had too many interests and soon moved on to other projects. Rudy also liked the idea of directing films. A lover of animals, he even thought some of returning to school and studying veterinary medicine. Whether this was serious or not one can't guess, but it does show the wide range of ideas he was tossing around and his lack of direction.

Rudy settled on opening his own nightclub and enlisted friends to back the endeavor. Among the co-owners were Bob Hope, Ken Murray and Tony Martin. The Pirates Den opened to much publicity in June

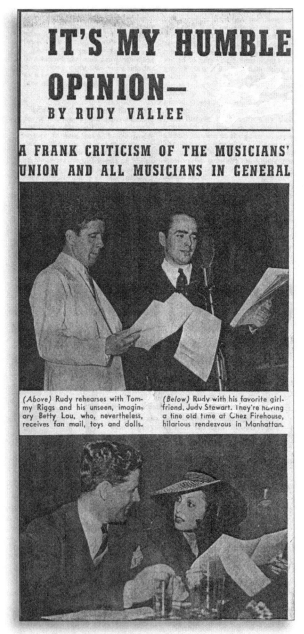

IT'S MY HUMBLE OPINION—

BY RUDY VALLEE

A FRANK CRITICISM OF THE MUSICIANS' UNION AND ALL MUSICIANS IN GENERAL

(Above) Rudy rehearses with Tommy Riggs and his unseen, imaginary Betty Lou, who, nevertheless, receives fan mail, toys and dolls.

(Below) Rudy with his favorite girl-friend, Judy Stewart. They're having a fine old time at Chez Firehouse, hilarious rendezvous in Manhattan.

One of Rudy's many columns — this one may have been accurate but hardly designed to win friends

INTERNATIONAL EVENTS, published Daily except Saturdays, Sundays and Holidays by INTERNATIONAL EVENTS, 430 N. Michigan Ave. Chicago, Ill-inois — By Subscription Only, $62.95 for two years.   Volume Two, Number 162, August 22nd, 1937   Entered as Second Class Matter, December 30, 1936, at the Post Office at Chicago, Illinois, under the act of March 2, 1879.

INTERNATIONAL EVENTS
THE WORLD'S NEWS IN PICTURES

VALLEE TO LEAVE RADIO AFTER TEN YEARS

NEW YORK — Rudy Vallee has announced his intention of leaving the air after the last performance of his current series, September 28, having completed ten years of unbroken broadcasting. Vallee had set a record for the longest association of a performer with a sponsor, having played for Standard Brands exclusively. His plans are still rather indefinite, but he is considering a South American trip, then a return to radio.

INTERNATIONAL EVENTS SPECIAL

FLASH

BRITISH MAIL MAY BE CARRIED BY ARMY PLANES

NAZI PAPER ACCUSES ROOSEVELT OF AROUSING POLES

FOR FURTHER PARTICULARS SEE YOUR NEWSPAPER

PRINTED IN U. S.

Rudy's announcement makes world news

With ever-present
canine companions

Rudy loved tennis —
but was a poor loser!

Rudy's breakfast party received great magazine coverage.

Rudy urging columnist Earl Wilson to have more than an olive!
Note Rudy's wall well-decorated with Vallée sheet music (photo: Gene Lester)

Rudy loved western outfits and enjoyed singing western songs. When Tom Mix died, Rudy had sung "Empty Saddles" at his funeral

RADIO STARS Turn PIRATES

EDGAR BERGEN, dining at the Pirates' Den on opening night with actress Joan Valerie, his steady date these days, wears a pirate's turban. "Very apt and very fitting" was Charlie McCarthy's terse comment

NEWEST Hollywood night spot—and one of interest to radio listeners for the part radio stars have in its operation—is the Pirates' Den. Backed largely by Rudy Vallee, Bing Crosby, Jimmie Fidler, Ken Murray, Bob Hope and Tony Martin, it is colorfully decorated with authentic pieces and replicas of pirate lore valued at more than $40,000. Waiters, attendants, check and cigarette girls wear pirates' costumes and refer to the paying guests as "wenches" in the case of women, "swabs" in the case of men. Floor show includes a slow-motion duel by pirates, exotic dance by a girl stowaway and an "almost" hanging which is postponed from night to night. These pictures were made on opening night.

DOROTHY LAMOUR screams for freedom as Ken Murray, left, and Rudy Vallee judge her effort. "Wenches" are imprisoned in the brig and freed only after they scream loud enough to satisfy the pirates

ABOVE: Mr. and Mrs. Jimmie Fidler dance at the opening, sponsored by Ann Lehr's Hollywood Guild. Proceeds went for charitable purposes

LEFT: Tossing bottles at iron pirates for prizes is another Den diversion. L. to r., Nancy Kelly, Gary Cooper, Ken Murray, Dorothy Lamour, Rudy Vallee

41

The Pirates Den was short-lived but lots of fun

**Rudy proudly graduated from Yale (note the ring),
but had a life-long affection for Maine**

1940. The opening was sponsored by the Hollywood Guild with the proceeds going to charity. Interest on the part of all waned quickly as other career commitments took precedence. The club closed soon after. It wasn't a total loss, however, as far as Rudy was concerned. It had been great fun and just the head-clearing diversion he needed.

Another radio show was not something he had in mind, but when the opportunity came he liked the new ideas. Not a talent show, this one

Swearing in, August 17, 1942 (courtesy: United States Coast Guard)

would be mostly comedy with interesting guest stars; and, of course, music by Vallée. Featured as an unlikely permanent guest was the great John Barrymore. Barrymore fans were divided on his appearing on the Vallée show. Many thought it demeaning for the Great Profile to lower himself to the comedy show. John, however, thoroughly enjoyed himself, despite declining health. Over time, both Lionel and Ethel Barrymore made appearances. What surprised Rudy was some of the negative reaction from a few listeners. Some were incensed by the sketches with a humorous take on American history. The show overall was highly successful and continued until Barrymore's death and Rudy's entry into the Coast Guard.

By 1941 war was raging in Europe and Asia. Actors along with fellow Americans were going into the military. At 39, Rudy was well over draft age, but longed to serve and considered volunteering for the Navy.

Coast Guard Band (courtesy: United States Coast Guard)

After all, he may have been only 15 at the time but was still a bona-fide ex-seaman. The opportunity came in another form. The Coast Guard was looking for someone to lead their 11th District Band. It was not to be just a band, but one which drew from the top musicians in the country. The men chosen had played with great bands, such as Ted Fio Rito, Paul Whiteman, Fred Waring, Benny Goodman, Glenn Miller and Freddy Martin, as well as the NBC Symphony. The Band Master must be an accomplished musician and one who, in plain words, would look great in uniform. Rudy fit the bill perfectly. His Navy experience was an added bonus. He was sworn in on August 17, 1942, and later declared it to be the best band he ever directed.

For the duration of the war he was Lieutenant Hubert Vallée, United

Band members sign in (courtesy: United States Coast Guard)

**Lieutenant Vallée with SPAR (courtesy:
United States Coast Guard)**

Dining with Jane

States Coast Guard. As a perfectionist who had run a tight ship with his Yankees and on his radio programs, Rudy was at times irked by the military red-tape and occasional inefficiency. Nevertheless, he was proud both of his service and the Coast Guard. His salary throughout the war was donated to the Coast Guard Fund and he remained a life-long supporter of the American military. The only symbol on his tombstone (per his request) would be that of the Coast Guard.

War or no, Rudy always found time for romance. When they started dating, Jane Greer seemed to Rudy his ideal woman –dark and glamorous. Theirs could be called the proverbial whirlwind courtship. And just as fast a marriage to divorce. Jane and Rudy were married with an elegant military guard. But in spite of the glamour studio buildup, Jane was at

**Jane Greer and Rudy on their wedding day, December 2, 1943
(courtesy: United States Coast Guard)**

heart still Bettyjane, the girl who loved to loaf in slacks and sandals — at odds with her husband who insisted his woman wear slinky dresses and 3-inch heels! Her mind was also on her career. Jane's marriage to Rudy alienated her mentor, Howard Hughes, which must also have caused her second thoughts. After only seven months of marriage, Jane and Rudy were divorced on July 27, 1944.

Rudy liked his women to focus on him first and their interests second. Probably this was the reason he was unsuccessful romantically with dedicated career women. His deep interest in Gene Tierney went nowhere, and he glumly admitted to friend Alan Dinehart that all Tierney had wanted was a good dance partner!

Rudy came back to a post-war Hollywood and a different music

Jane and Rudy — theirs was a short honeymoon

With musicians – Fenton Brothers, George and Joe

I'm singing Xmas carols
Atop the garden wall.
My dog however seems to feel
It isn't good at all.

Christmas Card c.1940

Gift from the State of Maine. Apprehensive lady is Rosemary Lane.

Sweater boy ad, 1940

With Helen Parrish on set of *Too Many Blondes*

scene. The new feminine idol was a skinny kid from Hoboken named Frank Sinatra. Movies were more serious and even comedies were different — the days of screwball comedies of the 1930s were over. Some former stars, such as Clark Gable, Tyrone Power, Glenn Ford and others, resumed movie-star status. Some moved into character roles or went into retirement. Television, that new rage, reignited the careers of Ronald Reagan and Robert Montgomery. Dick Powell, whose boyish manner charmed filmgoers in 1930s musicals, made a smooth transition to the detective-mystery genre.

For Rudy, things were not so easy. After a few 1930s films he never managed to make it big as a romantic movie star. Radio had been his

Ellen Drew, RV and Minna Gombell on set of *Man Alive*

life but now it seemed everyone was enamored by television. In the early days, as television was being developed, Rudy had been excited. He saw it as a perfect medium for his special talent of music and comedy. Instead, he was offered another radio show. Sponsored by Drene Shampoo, this half-hour show would run from September 1944 to June 1946. It was a great show with an impressive list of guest stars. With its demise Rudy moved to another sponsor, Philip Morris, but this was a short-lived six months.

Movie roles still came his way and the films, for the most part, were first-class, but his character was nearly always the same — that of the stuffy suitor. Rudy did enjoy working at Republic Studios and making *The Fabulous Suzanne* (1946) and *I Remember Mama* for RKO (1948). Also, great fun was had in the making of *So This is New York* (United

I Remember Mama gave Rudy one of his more satisfying
roles and one in which he received fine reviews

With Betty Grable. They co-starred in *The Beautiful Blonde from Bashful Bend*

Artists, 1948). Most of the rest he could have practically played without looking at a script, the characters were so frustratingly similar. The only enjoyable thing about *The Beautiful Blonde from Bashful Bend* was getting to work with longtime friend Betty Grable.

In 1955 Rudy traveled to Paris to play himself in United Artists' *Gentlemen Marry Brunettes*. Traveling from the airport to the hotel, he shared a limo with Alan Young. Alan had become acquainted with Rudy after having guested on his radio show. Guests on the show were always invited back to the Vallée's for refreshments and to listen to the show just performed. He was then taken on a tour of Rudy's basement, which Alan remembered as a "library/ museum/ junkyard!" During the ride, which took an hour, Alan recalled that Rudy "would voice his opinion on everything and everybody, living or dead. While one might disagree with his opinions, you had to admire his verbiage." Rudy's penchant for

With fellow "musicians" Shemp Howard, Eddie Quillan and Lon Chaney, Jr.

lecturing either amused or irritated. Alan was amused and enjoyed working with him.

In all, from 1929 to 1955, Rudy made 27 feature films. After that date, there were minor roles and a number of exploitative films, with only one exception: *How to Succeed in Business Without Really Trying*. These years, from 1940 to the mid-'50s, were the most fun and ones with the happiest memories. There were disappointments, to be sure, and the usual broken romances, but nothing like the grinding work and heartbreak of the 1930s — ironically the decade he was on top of the world as one of the world's most famous men and a romantic idol to millions.

Looking back, Rudy remembered 1947 as one of his best years. His good luck came in the form of a beautiful 17-year-old redhead named

Rudy loved being surrounded by beautiful women, here with Ann Miller, Joan Merrill and Rosemary Lane. Ann remembers RV "as a very sweet man."

With brother Bill, Bill's wife, Charles Vallée and dad's date (from Arkansas?)

(courtesy: Eleanor Vallée)

(courtesy: Eleanor Vallée)

Eleanor Norris. All visions of dark beauties vanished, and, on September 3, 1948, the 48-year-old Rudy married his 18-year-old love. No one in the world gave the marriage a chance, and not only because of the age difference. Rudy's record was not exactly encouraging. Despite all the odds, their marriage and love would last his lifetime. In the ensuing years as his fame waned, Ellie would be a constant source of encouragement and love. In this regard he fared better than many has-been idols.

Last Hurrah

Nothing irritated Rudy more than reports of his "comeback." It seemed every time he appeared as a guest on a television show or with a live performance at a club, someone would write a story about a Rudy Vallée comeback. As Rudy would say, "I've never been anywhere."

Nevertheless, the point of concentration he had in the 1920s and 1930s was obviously lost. Now he had too many interests. The television specials he was so uniquely equipped for never came his way. Reasons are many — but the main one being his own sometimes caustic personality. Perhaps he had worked too hard early on and the urge to repeat was not there. Despite everything, he was enjoying life and exploring all kinds of possibilities. Fine perhaps for a 20-year-old, but when you are 50 and trying to ignite your career it can be fatal.

On the road with poodles Pom-Pom and Mimi

A break from work the Vallées took a cruise – here hamming it up in Hong Kong

It is true he seemed to be working regularly, but not always as a star, so it was often overlooked. He appeared seven times on Ed Sullivan's *Toast of the Town*, hoping it would lead to his own variety show, and was disappointed when there were no permanent offers.

What he really hoped for was a talk show — one in which he could choose the guests. There would be no limit on subjects or censorship of views. No studio executive would agree to those terms so nothing came of it. Later, such a show did air, hosted by Jack Paar, whom Rudy greatly admired.

There were the sitcom and game shows (he was not fond of the latter), which came along during the 1950s. Of special note was the stage show *Jenny Kissed Me*. It played coast to coast for 19 weeks to rave reviews. The stage had definitely become Rudy's medium and one wonders why he didn't more actively pursue good projects of this kind.

But there were the club dates. It was nothing like the early days when he drew enormous crowds and the pay was huge. Now he worked mainly on a house percentage — but he and Ellie were enjoying themselves and

Silver Tip, a magnificent home with a glorious view built in the 1930s
by actress Ann Harding. Rudy enlarged it to include tennis courts
and pool. Sadly, when it was sold, the owner immediately had it
torn down, a priceless piece of Hollywood history forever lost

traveling. The only really sad times were on the occasion of Ellie's two
miscarriages — neither of which Rudy mentions in his memoirs, even the
tell-all *Let the Chips Fall*. He was always careful to hide his pain, perhaps
a hangover from the media frenzy with Fay.

Rudy hated the idea of growing old. He detested elderly fans that
came up to inform him of how they had loved him "when they were
young!" He had this love/hate relationship with the past. Often, Rudy
would say how the past was best forgotten and one must look ahead.

He once ruefully remarked that "somebody up there doesn't like me."
There was more truth than fiction in that statement. Rudy had never been

Home at Silver Tip. Not enough space was allowed for cars turning around so the turntable was installed. Instructions for using it were posted: "Drive middle of car into MIDDLE of turntable. Shut off motor. Put car in GEAR. Pull handbrake lightly. Place hands on left front mudguard then PUSH LIKE HELL!]

Christmas at Silver Tip

a back-slapper, cozy-up-to kind of person. It wasn't part of his nature and unfortunately often in show business that type gets the calls and privileges. He couldn't have abided the hangers-on or fawning entourages that characterize the lives of so many other legends. The sorest part of all was in the end the lack of general recognition as one of the great radio pioneers.

But he had his vast collection of memorabilia attesting to the phenomenon that was Rudy Vallée from 1925 to 1940. This collection of memorabilia was one of the greatest ever compiled by an entertainer. He saved everything, delighting in giving guests a tour of his own "museum." Of course, the tour would include listening to some vintage Vallée recordings.

Rudy loved to recall all the great talents he had introduced and

With Vallée household

helped along the way. He liked them to remember it also, and held a grudge against persons he thought had forgotten. When Kate Smith was seriously ill, her friends planned a television tribute and contacted old friends and colleagues to take part. Rudy was one of those receiving an

During his "mod" phase (courtesy: Ed Colbert)

At premiere of *How to Succeed in Business*
Without Really Trying **(courtesy: Ed Colbert)**

invitation. He might have ignored it or written a small decline, but the Vallée temper took hold. The note he wrote was mean spirited as he declared that Kate deserved her affliction. Rudy liked to blame those lapses in self-discipline to his Irish-French genes — a way to avoid an apology perhaps.

When it seemed as if nothing great was going to come along again, Rudy received a call from Abe Burrows. Burrows had co-authored a play based on the satiric book, *How to Succeed in Business Without Really Trying.* There was a part for Rudy if he was available. Rudy was delighted with the prospect, but there were some hitches. Burrows' partners weren't sure if Vallée's voice was strong enough for a musical of this sort. Again, radio came to Rudy's rescue. A tiny microphone transmitter concealed in his vest pocket carried his voice to the theatre sound system.

The other question was about his age. Some backers really had no idea who he was and questioned whether the 60-something Vallée could stand the rigors of the theatre run. Despite questions and, at times, friction, especially between Rudy (those Irish-French genes!) and Frank Loesser, Rudy was not to be deprived of this, his best stage role. As it turned out, he was the only member of the cast during its long run not to miss a day for illness. Opening night, Rudy, as J.B. Biggley, brought down the house with his rendition of "Grand Old Ivy." When the play was made into a movie no one could imagine anyone else as J.B. Though the film can't compare to the stage, still fans can enjoy seeing Rudy in one of his greatest roles.

The last stage production Rudy appeared in, *Once Upon a Mattress* (1973), was not a pleasant one. Whatever the reasons, cast members found him difficult. And it must be admitted that he was becoming more irritable.

Though nothing could quite top *How to Succeed*, a few roles in sitcoms came along, and some great radio interviews.

On February 11, 1986, Rudy checked into the Cedars-Sinai Medical

As J.B. Biggley

Once Upon a Mattress playbill (courtesy: Lucie Arnaz)

**Frank Bresee was the host as well as creator of *The Golden Days of Radio*.
He often welcomed Rudy as an in-person guest as well as frequently
using excerpts from his past radio programs (courtesy: Frank Bresee)**

Center for an operation of his esophagus. He was in fine spirits and opti-
mistic, but being Rudy he insisted on an updated will and wrote it before
the operation. Simply put, everything would go to Ellie and the public
would eventually be surprised at the modest fortune. Rudy once admitted that his "legendary millions are just that — legendary." Like many
Vallée myths, the fortune was like the stories of his parsimony. It is true he
could be cheap about small things, but (lesser-known) amazingly generous in the larger. The operation took 13 hours and Rudy came through
fine. He was well on his way to recovery when a week later he received a
medication causing an allergic reaction and suffered a stroke.

During his final months, friends visited and reminisced about the old

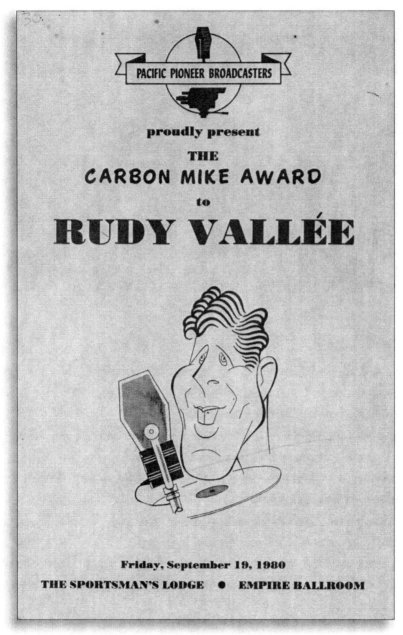

Pacific Pioneer Broadcasters presented their award to
Rudy. His comment: "It's about time."

Ellie and Rudy

days and allowed Ellie to have some rest. But usually Rudy wanted her near, so she stayed by his side, humoring him when necessary by agreeing to plans she knew were not reasonable.

In July they received an invitation from President Reagan to be his guest at the unveiling of the renewed Statue of Liberty. The Vallées, of course, knew attending was not possible, but settled in front of the television to watch the ceremonies.

Rudy took Ellie's hand, saying quietly, "I would like to be there, you know I like a party." He gave a sigh and was gone.

Years later, Eleanor, in an interview, was asked what it had been like living with Rudy Vallée. The answer could have summed up his entire life: "It was one long love song."

Under the Footlights

1. **Rudy Vallée and the Connecticut Yankees** – On Stage (1928)
    Keith's 81st Street Theatre: Rudy Vallée and the Connecticut
    Yankees
    Opening night traffic-stopping mobs of fans led immediately to a
    lengthier Paramount engagement.

2. **Rudy Vallée and the Connecticut Yankees** – On Stage
    (1928-1929) Palace Theatre, Manhattan and Paramount Theatre,
    Brooklyn, 18 months.
    At this time he would share the stage with other up-and-coming per-
    formers such as Milton Berle and George Jessel.
    Rudy and his band kept up an amazingly hectic pace, performing
    at both theatres on the same afternoon, dashing from one to the other,
    while continuing his nightclub commitment as well.

3. *George White's Scandals* (1931) Apollo Theatre, Opening:
    September 14, 1931 Closing: March 1932 202 performances
    George White (producer/director/choreographer), Ray Henderson
    (music), Lew Brown (Lyrics), Lew Brown, Irving Caesar, George White
    (sketches). Cast: Rudy Vallée, Ethel Merman, Willie and Eugene How-

ard, Everett Marshall, Ethel Barrymore Colt, Ray Bolger, Alice Faye with (rest of opening night cast): Joan Abbott, Jane Alden, Barbara Blair, Hazel Biffinger, Fred Manatt, The Gale Quadruplets, The Loomis Sisters, Alice Frohman, Ross McLean, Peggy Moseley.

Songs include: "Life is Just a Bowl of Cherries," "The Thrill Is Gone," "This is the Mrs.," "Ladies and Gentlemen, That's Love," "That's Why Darkies Were Born," "My Song."

4. *George White's Scandals* (1935) New Amsterdam Theatre, Opening: December 25, 1935 Closing: March 28, 1936 110 performances

George White (producer/director), Ray Henderson (music), Jack Yellin (lyrics), Conrad Salinger, Russell Bennett (orchestration), George

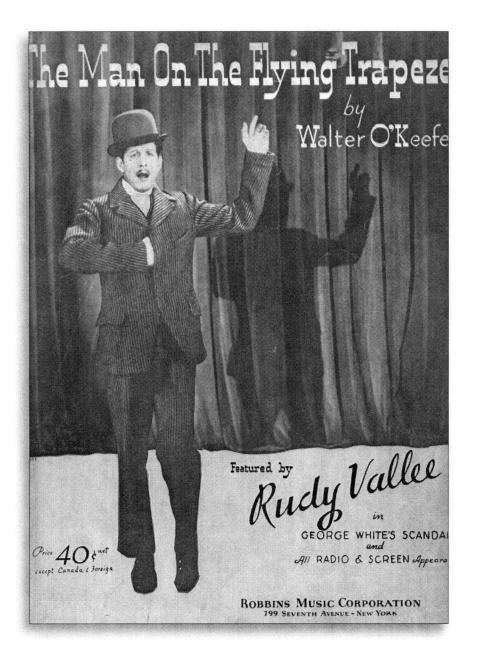

New Bedford
Lodge
No. 73
B. P. O. Elks

PRESENTS

RUDY VALLEE
and His Connecticut Yankees
with ALICE FAYE
FEATURING A VARIETY PROGRAM
AT LINCOLN PARK
FRIDAY EVENING, SEPTEMBER 8TH
Benefit Elk's Christmas Basket Fund

Dancing 8 - 1   ADMISSION $1.00-No Tax

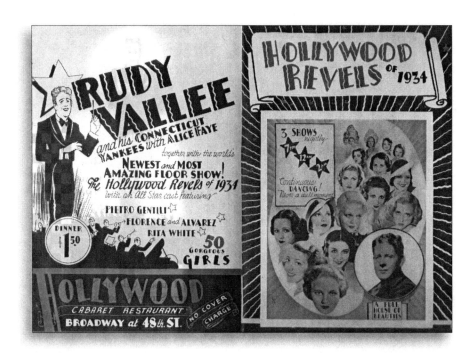

White, William Wells, Howard Shiebler (sketches). Cast: Rudy Vallée, Cliff Edwards, Bert Lahr, Gracie Barrie, Hal Forde, Willie and Eugene Howard, Lois Eckhart, Estelle Jayne, Richard Lane, Claire McQuillen, with (rest of opening night cast): The George White Girls, The Apollo Quartet, Helene Miller, Jane Cooper, Peggy Moseley, Edna Page.

Songs include: "The (Daring Young) Man on the Flying Trapeze," "I'm the Fellow Who Loves You."

5. *The Man in Possession* (1938) Paper Mill Playhouse, Milburn, N.J.

Opening: September 25, 1938

Cast: Rudy Vallée, Viola Roache, Enid Markey, Crahan Denton, Paul Ballantyne, Philippa Bevans, Natalie Hall, John Clarke, John Halloran, Edward Tarvey.

First opening with Leslie Banks in 1930, by 1938 the plotline was

considered passé. After a scathing review by Brooks Atkinson, the 1938 version with Rudy closed quickly.

6. ***Ken Murray's Blackouts*** (1942-1948) El Capitan Theatre, Vine Street, Hollywood, California
   A popular variety stage show featuring "unannounced" guest stars. Rudy Vallée was a frequent guest.

WHAT THE MOVIE STARS SAY
about Ken Murray's "Blackouts"

EDDIE CANTOR

"I agree with Mary Pickford—it's a great morale builder and a swell show."

MARY PICKFORD

"I am delighted with the show. It's the best morale booster in town. I've seen it six times — hope it runs indefinitely."

JACK BENNY

"It's just a question of time—everybody's got to see this show. It's tops!"

ANN SHERIDAN

"If a show can have oomph, you've got it. Delightful entertainment."

FRED ASTAIRE

"I'm crazy about your show, Ken. It's wonderful!"

ALAN LADD

"You're the killer, Ken—not me. A great show!"

MICKEY ROONEY

"Twice for me—and I'll be back again. A great show!"

JIMMY DURANTE

"It's terrific . . . it's colossal . . . it's gigantic. Boy, what a show!"

ROBERT YOUNG

"Yes, it's true what they say of Ken Murray; he's tops."

VAN HEFLIN

"Definitely a show that must be rated with the top-notchers of all time."

SONJA HEINE

"It looks as though it will go on forever—and that's great for everybody."

Sally Fraser as Jenny and Rudy as Father Moynihan

7. *Jenny Kissed Me* (1954) (1956) written by Jean Kerr

A charming story about a young 18-year-old girl who comes to live in the household of a priest. The plot revolves around Father Moynihan's attempt to match Jenny with a suitable young man. Jenny, however, has from the first, set her eyes on an older man who wins the day.

The play ran for 12 weeks in various straw-hat playhouses in and around Maine, starring Lee Remick as Jenny and Rudy Vallée as Father Moynihan. The same cast also toured 19 weeks coast to coast, receiving

rave notices. In 1956 the play was revived for a successful run at the Pasadena Playhouse, California. Sally Fraser played the title character, with Rudy reprising his role.

8. *Hadacol All-Star Caravan Tour*
Hadacol Caravan was billed as the last of the big-time medicine shows that touted a "vitamin" mixture. Later declared illegal because of its 24% alcohol content, Rudy Vallée was only one of many celebrities who marketed the product. Other big-name stars included James Cagney, Bob Hope, Lucille Ball, George Burns and Gracie Allen, Judy Garland, Milton Berle, Hank Williams, Jack Dempsey, Dorothy Lamour, Minnie Pearl, Mickey Rooney, Chico and Groucho Marx, Carmen Miranda and Cesar Romero.

9. *How to Succeed in Business Without Really Trying* (1961) 46th Street Theatre, Preview: October 12, 1961 Opening: October 14, 1961 Closing: March 6, 1965 1417 performances
Abe Burrows (director), Bob Fosse, Hugh Lambert (choreographers), Cy Feuer, Ernest Martin (producers), Frank Loesser (music/lyrics), Abe Burrows, Jack Weinstock, Willie Gilbert (book), based on the book by Shepherd Mead. Cast: Robert Morse (J. Pierrepont Finch), Rudy Vallée (J.B. Biggley), Virginia Martin (Hedy La Rue), Charles Nelson Reilly (Bud Frump), Bonnie Scott (Rosemary Pilkington), Ruth Kobart (Miss Jones), Sammy Smith (Mr. Twimble).
Songs include: "Coffee Break," "The Company Way," "A Secretary is Not a Toy," "Grand Old Ivy," "Paris Original," "Rosemary," "I Believe in You," "Brotherhood of Man."

10. *Once Upon a Mattress* (1973) Kenley Players Dayton & Columbus, Ohio, summer stock
Leslie Cutler (director), John DeMain (musical director), Mary

**Cast of *Once Upon a Mattress*. Top: Kay Medford, Lucie Arnaz, RV
bottom: Ed Evanko, Dean Dittman (courtesy: Lucie Arnaz)**

REMARKS TO HECKLERS

IF YOU DISAPPEAR SUDDENLY, IT COULDN'T HAPPEN TO A NICER GUY.

I DON'T KNOW WHAT I'D DO WITHOUT YOU, BUT I'D RATHER.

WILL SOMEBODY AT   TABLE PLEASE OPEN THE BOTTLE SO
HE CAN FIND HIS WAY BACK.

LET'S PLAY HORSEY. I'LL PLAY THE FRONT PART, AND YOU STAY
AS SWEET AS YOU ARE.

YOU WOULDN'T LIKE IT IF I CAME WHERE YOU WORKED AND TURNED OUT
THE RED LIGHT.

I WOULD HAVE SENT YOU A PRESENT, BUT THERE'S NO WAY OF
WRAPPING UP A BRONX CHEER.

WHEN HAVING DIFFICULTY IN A CITY: I WASN'T BORN HERE, BUT I'M
SURE DYING HERE.

TO A BALD-HEADED MAN: THAT GUY BLEW HIS TOP.

WHY DON'T YOU TAKE THE 1:30 BROOM OUT OF TOWN?

IF YOU WANT THE FLOOR SO MUCH, WHY DON'T YOU CRAWL BACK UNDER IT?

CAN I DROP YOU OFF SOMEWHERE? OFF THE GEORGE WASHINGTON
BRIDGE, FOR INSTANCE?

TO A DRUNK: AW, CLIMB BACK INTO YOUR FLASK.

IF I EVER BURP: WHAT DO YOU EXPECT, CHIMES?

LOOK, WHY DON'T YOU BE QUIET AND FIND HOW BAD I REALLY CAN BE?

TO ANOTHER DRUNK: HE'LL SOBER UP WHEN HE GETS THE CHECK.

TO A BALD-HEADED RIBBER: DIDN'T I SHOOT YOU INTO THE SIDE
POCKET SOMEPLACE?

I KNOW THERE'S AN AUDIENCE OUT THERE--I CAN HEAR YOU BREATHING.

TO A RIBBER WITH A VERY UNATTRACTIVE APPEARANCE OR VOICE:
IF I NEED A STOOGE, I'LL GET ONE WITH A COLLEGE EDUCATION.

YOU NOW HAVE 32 TEETH. WOULD YOU LIKE TO TRY FOR NONE?

THERE'S A GUY WITH A BRAIN MARKED 'TILT'.

WHEN DO YOU LET THE AIR OUT OF YOUR HEAD?

Rudy's "adlibs" to hecklers

Rogers (music), Marshall Barer (lyrics), Leo Muller (choreographer), book by Jay Thompson, Marshall Barer and Dean Fuller. Cast: Lucie Arnaz (Princess Winnifred the Woebegone), Rudy Vallée (King Sextimus the Silent), Kay Medford (Queen Aggravain), Christine Andreas (Lady Larken), Ed Evanko (Sir Harry), Don Amendolia (Prince Dauntless), Dean Dittman (the Minstrel), Frank Echols (the Wizard), J.J. Jepson (the Jester).

A re-telling of the fairy tale *The Princess and the Pea*, with Lucie Arnaz in the role originated on Broadway by Carol Burnett.

It is impossible to list all Rudy's club appearances. There are literally hundreds, on two continents; from the likes of those London Savoy engagements, the elegant *Hollywood Revels*, up to the 1960s stand-up comedy routines.

REMARKS TO HECKLERS   -2-

WHEN SOMEBODY HISSES ME: THERE ARE ONLY THREE THINGS THAT HISS--A GOOSE, A SNAKE, AND A FOOL. COME FORTH AND BE IDENTIFIED.

TO A NOISY DRUNK: MAY I SAY THAT I ENJOYED YOU IN THE LOST WEEKEND?

GO STICK YOUR HEAD OUT OF A WINDOW--FEET FIRST.

WHY DON'T YOU TAKE A LONG WALK ON A SHORT PIER.

TO A VERY DESPICABLE CHARACTER: THERE'S THE MAIN REASON FOR TWIN BEDS.

ONLY GOD CAN MAKE A TREE, BUT IT TOOK YOUR PARENTS TO MAKE THE SAP.

WHEN YOUR FACE COMES TO A HEAD, HAVE IT LANCED.

IS THIS AN AUDIENCE, OR A JURY?

PLEASE, YOU ARE ANNOYING THE MAN I LOVE.

TO A MAN WHO'S SEATED ALL ALONE: I SEE YOU'RE HERE WITH ALL YOUR FRIENDS.

I NEVER FORGET A FACE, BUT IN YOUR CASE I'LL MAKE AN EXCEPTION.

INSTEAD OF THE BEER YOU HAVE, HAVE THE BARTENDER PUT THE HEAD ON YOU.

IF YOU HAVE YOUR LIFE TO LIVE OVER AGAIN, DON'T DO IT.

DON'T LOOK NOW, BUT THERE'S A DOPE STANDING IN YOUR SHOES.

TOO BAD BIRTH CONTROL ISN'T RETROACTIVE.

WHO DOES THE EMBALMING HERE?

WHY DON'T YOU GO OUT AND BUY A CAR AND HAVE AN ACCIDENT?

AT A COLLEGE DINNER: HE HAS A B.A. DEGREE. HE MASTERED THE FIRST TWO LETTERS OF THE ALPHABET.

HIS MOTHER SENT HIS PICTURE TO RIPLEY, AND IT CAME BACK MARKED 'I DON'T BELIEVE IT'.

BETTY CO-ED

COLLEGIATE SWEETHEART SONG

FOX TROT

FISCHER "NU-STYLE" MULTI-PART EDITION

Including Solos or Duets for SAXOPHONES *And Other E♭ & B♭ Instruments*

TENOR BANJO

HAWAIIAN GUITAR

Arranged as Solo or Duet for BANJO *and* GUITAR

Also for UKULELE

ALL IN ONE

Featured by RUDY VALLÉE

Words & Music by PAUL FOGARTY and RUDY VALLÉE

Published by CARL FISCHER, INC.

COOPER SQUARE, NEW YORK.

Your Listening Pleasure

Despite the fact that Rudy wrote quite a few songs he denied being a "songwriter"– that title he believed belonged to the professionals. Also, he admitted adding his name to several songs of which he contributed little. With his usual bluntness, he said singers of the songs deserved "some of the action."

"Deep Night" RV, Charlie Henderson. Victor Records, 2/6/29.

"I'm Still Caring" RV, John Klenner. Victor Records, 3/15/29.

"Me Queres?" (a.k.a. "Do You Love Me?") RV, Carlos Cobian (sung in both Spanish and English), Victor Records, 5/5/29.

"I Love the Moon" Paul Rubens (American version by RV). Victor Records, 8/7/29.

"The Stein Song" E.A. Fenstad, Lincoln Colcord (revision by RV). Victor Records, 2/10/30.

"Kitty from Kansas City" RV, Harry Rose, Jesse Greer, George Bronson. Victor Records, 4/8/30.

"Betty Co-Ed" RV, Paul Fogarty. Victor Records, 6/25/30.

"Forgive Me" RV, James A. Morcaldi. Victor Records, 6/25/30.

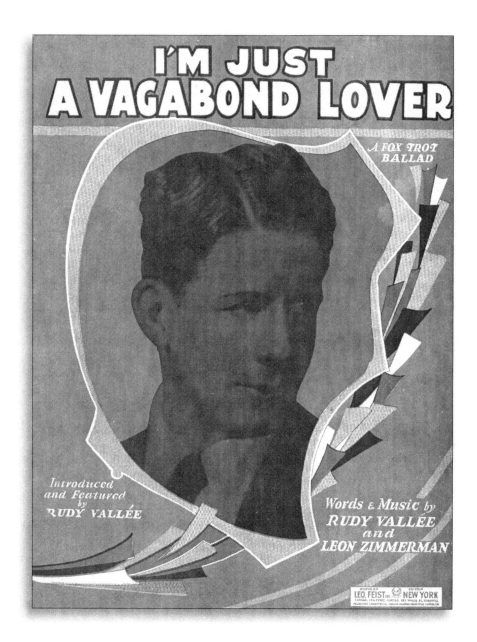

STEIN SONG

(UNIVERSITY OF MAINE)

A New Arrangement by RUDY VALLÉE

for
VOICE AND PIANO

Music by
E. A. FENSTAD

Arrangement by
A. W. SPRAGUE

Words by
LINCOLN COLCORD

Also Published

Vocal Orchestration
Special Dance Orchestration
Band Arrangement

CARL FISCHER, INC.
. . . . Cooper Square, NEW YORK

V 1117

"Magic of the Moonlight" RV, Ian Campbell. Victor Records, 7/8/30.

"When Vagabond Dreams Come True" RV. Victor Records, 7/16/30.

"The Golden West, A Silvery Nest, and You" RV. Victor Records, 7/16/30.

"She Loves Me Just the Same" RV, Paul Fogarty, Joe Sanders. Victor Records, 10/13/30.

"To the Legion" RV, Richard C. Jones. Victor Records, 11/5/30.

"The Song of the Navy" RV, Byron Gay, Haven Gillespie. Victor Records, 11/5/30.

"My Cigarette Lady" RV, Carroll Gibbons. Victor Records, 4/8/31.

"Two Little Blue Eyes" RV, John Jacob Loeb, Paul Francis Webster. Victor Records, 4/15/31.

"Old Man Harlem" RV, Hoagy Carmichael. Victor Records, 2/24/33.

"Somewhere in Your Heart" RV, Bert Van Cleve, Guy B. Wood. Victor Records, 8/6/34

"Just an Old Banjo" RV, J. Rosamund Johnson, Bartley Costello. Victor Records, 8/6/34.

"The Drunkard Song" (a.k.a. "There's a Tavern in the Town") Traditional Cornish folk song (revision by RV). Victor Records, 9/7/34.

"I'm Just a Vagabond Lover" RV, Leon Zimmerman. Victor Records, 7/17/35.

"All Right, All Right, All Right" RV, Dave Franklin. Song dedicated to radio pioneer Major Edward Bowes, the title being the catch phrase on Bowes' *Amateur Hour* program. First sung by RV on the NBC's *Fleischmann Hour* on 3/12/36.

"The Whiffenpoof Song" Meade Minnigerode, George Pomeroy, Tod Galloway (revision by RV, with special lyrics by Moss Hart). Warner-Brunswick Corporation, 10/16/36.

"Vieni, Vieni" George Koger, H. Varna, Vincent Scotto (revision by RV). English Columbia Records, London, 5/14/37.

"Don't Play with Fire" RV, Clifford Grey, Antonio Moretti, Mario Moretti. Victor Recording Company, 7/2/37.

"The Old Sow Song" RV, Cyril Smith, Elliot Daniel. Victor Recording Company, 7/2/37.

"Oh! Ma-Ma!" Paolo Citorello (revision by RV). Victor Records, 4/13/38.

"Phil the Fluter's Ball" W.P. French (American version by RV). Victor Records, 6/10/38.

"You Took Me Out of This World" RV, Milton Berle, Irving Actman, George R. Brown. Decca Records, 7/27/39.

"Where To?" (Originally titled "Taxi Man") RV, Jack Osterman, Elliot Daniel, Elliot Jacoby. Private recording, c.1940.

"I'll Make Love the Most Important Occupation if You Will Vote For Me" RV, Abe Burrows, Elliot Daniel. *The Sealtest Show Presents Rudy Vallée*, 10/31/40.

"That Woman of Mine" RV, Canfield & Plumstead. Maestro Music Records, c.1945-46.

"Alouetta" Traditional French folk song (revision by RV). Enterprise Records, c.1946.

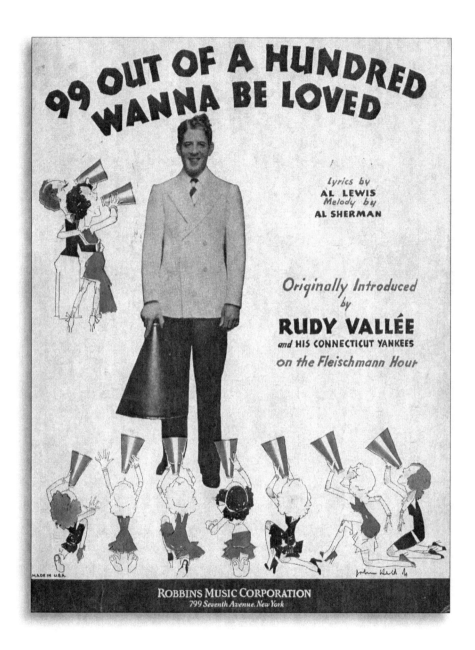

"You Know What I Mean" RV, Glazier. Private recording, spring 1946.

Rudy recorded more than 600 songs. These were his greatest hits, as listed under the original label.

"As Time Goes By" Herman Hupfeld. Victor Records, 7/25/31.

"All the Things You Are" Jerome Kern, Oscar Hammerstein II. Warner Bros. & 20th Century-Fox Studios recording session, c.1943.

"Betty Co-Ed" RV, Paul Fogarty. Victor Records, 6/25/30.

"Brother, Can You Spare a Dime?" Jay Gorney, E.Y. Harburg. Columbia Records, 10/27/32.

"Dancing in the Moonlight" Walter Donaldson, Gus Kahn. Victor Records, 2/2/34.

"Deep Night" RV, Charlie Henderson. Victor Records, 2/6/29.

"Doin' the Raccoon" Raymond Klages, J. Fred Coots. Harmony Records, 10/10/28.

"The Drunkard Song" (a.k.a. "There's a Tavern in the Town") Traditional Cornish folk song (revision by RV). Victor Records, 9/7/34.

"Empty Saddles" Billy Hill, J. Keirn Brennan. Warner-Brunswick Corporation, 5/27/36.

"Ev'ry Day" Sammy Fain, Irving Kahal. Victor Records, 12/24/34.

"The Glory of Love" Billy Hill. Warner-Brunswick Corporation, 4/16/36.

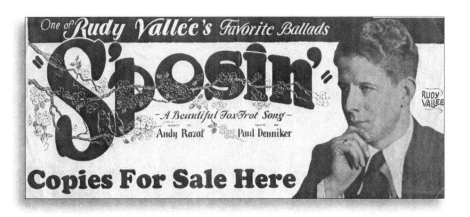

"Good Green Acres of Home" Sammy Fain, Irving Kahal. Victor Records, 12/7/34.

"Goodnight Sweetheart" Ray Noble. Victor Records, 7/17/35.

"Harbor Lights" Hugh Williams, Jimmy Kennedy. Victor Recording Company, 7/2/37.

"Heigh Ho! Ev'rybody, Heigh Ho!" Harry M. Woods. Victor Records, 6/3/29.

"I Didn't Know What Time it Was" Lorenz Hart, Richard Rodgers. Electro-Vox Studios, private recording, c.1940.

"I Poured My Heart into a Song" Irving Berlin. 20th Century-Fox Studios, *Second Fiddle* (film), early 1939.

"If I Had a Girl Like You" Louis W. McDermott. Victor Records, 4/30/30.

"If I Had You" Ted Shapiro, Jimmy Campbell, Reginald Connelly. Harmony Records, 1/10/29.

"I'm Just a Vagabond Lover" RV, Leon Zimmerman. Victor Records, 7/17/35.

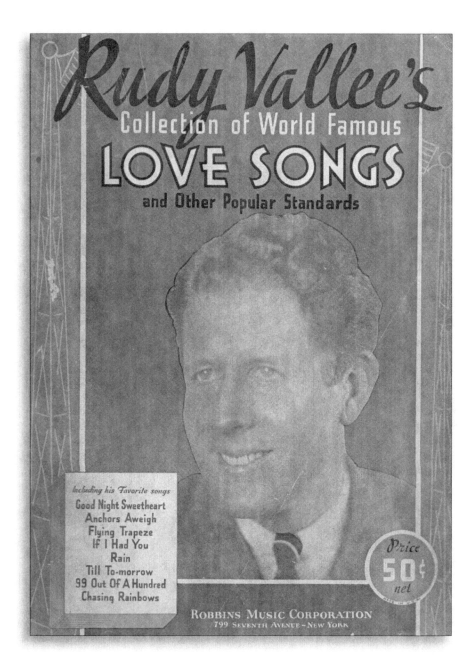

"Is it True What They Say About Dixie?" Gerald Marks, Irving Caesar, Sonny Lerner. Victor Records, 2/24/36.

"I've Got to Sing a Torch Song" Harry Warren, Al Dubin. Columbia Records, 4/17/33.

"Kitty from Kansas City" RV, Harry Rose, Jesse Greer, George Bronson. Victor Records, 4/8/30.

"Let's Do it (Let's Fall in Love)" Cole Porter. Harmony Records,   12/12/28.

"Let's Put Out the Lights (and Go to Sleep)" Herman Hupfeld. Columbia Records, 9/9/32.

"Life is Just a Bowl of Cherries" Lew Brown, Ray Henderson. Victor Records, 8/7/31.

"A Little Kiss Each Morning, a Little Kiss Each Night" Harry M. Woods. Victor Records, 11/6/29.

"Love is the Sweetest Thing" Ray Noble. Bluebird Records, 9/6/33.

"Mad Dogs and Englishmen" Noel Coward. Victor Record Company, 8/11/37.

"The Man on the Flying Trapeze," based on old English song "The Flying Trapeze" George Leybourne (written/introduced 1868), Walter O'Keefe (revised/introduced this version). Victor Records, 8/6/34.

"My Blue Heaven" Walter Donaldson. Viva Records, c.1966.

"My Dancing Lady" Jimmy McHugh, Dorothy Fields. Victor Records, 11/8/33.

"My Time is Your Time" Eric Little, Leo Dance. Victor Records, 2/12/39.

"Page Miss Glory" Al Dubin, Harry Warren. Victor Records, 7/17/35.

"A Pretty Girl is Like a Melody" Irving Berlin. Victor Records, 12/24/34.

"Say it Isn't So" Irving Berlin. Columbia Records. 9/9/32.

"The Song I Love" Con Conrad, Lew Brown, Buddy DeSylva, Ray Henderson. Harmony Records, 12/12/28.

"S'posin'" Andy Razaf, Paul Denniker. Victor Records, 4/29/29.

"Star Dust" Hoagy Carmichael, Mitchell Parish. Warner Bros. & 20th Century-Fox Studios recording session, c.1943.

"The Stein Song" E.A. Fenstad, Lincoln Colcord (revision by RV). Victor Records, 2/10/30.

"Sweetheart of All My Dreams" Art Fitch, Kay Fitch, Bert Lown.   Harmony Records, 10/10/28

"Sweet Music" Al Dubin, Harry Warren. Victor Records, 12/7/34.

"Take Me Back to My Boots and Saddle" Teddy Powell, Walter Samuels, Leonard Whitcup. Victor Record Company, 8/11/37.

"These Foolish Things Remind Me of You" Holt Marvell, Jack Strahey, Harry Link. Warner-Brunswick Corporation, 5/27/36.

"This is the Mrs." Lew Brown, Ray Henderson. Victor Records, 8/7/31.

"Vieni, Vieni" George Koger, H. Varna, Vincent Scotto (revision by RV). English Columbia Records, London, 5/14/37.

"Was That the Human Thing to Do?" Sammy Fain, Joe Young. Durium Products Incorporated, 2/32.

"The Way You Look Tonight" Dorothy Fields, Jerome Kern. Warner-Brunswick Corporation, 7/30/36.

"Weary River" Grant Clarke, Louis Silvers. Victor Records, 2/6/29.

"The Whiffenpoof Song" Meade Minnigerode, George Pomeroy, Tod Galloway (revision by RV, with special lyrics by Moss Hart). Warner-Brunswick Corporation, 10/16/36.

Rudy signed and returned this sheet music
to a fan and included this interesting note

"You Oughta Be in Pictures" Dana Suesse, Ed Heyman. Victor Records, 3/5/34.

"You Took Me Out of This World" RV, Milton Berle, Irving Actman, George R. Brown. Decca Records, 7/27/39.

"You'll Do it Someday (So Why Not Now?)" Allie Wrubel. Columbia Recording Studios, 3/26/26.

"You're Driving Me Crazy! (What Did I Do?)" Walter Donaldson. Victor Records, 11/10/30.

Over the Airwaves

1. Herbert's Blue-White Diamonds

Remote from the Heigh-Ho Club on Sundays, beginning February 1928, sponsored by Herbert's Blue-White Diamonds. After being carried on local stations WABC, WMCA and WOR for about a year, Rudy was ready for a national audience.

2-3. *The Fleischmann Hour/The Royal Gelatin Hour*

The Fleischmann Hour, one of the first great variety hours, started on NBC in the fall of 1929 and was the top-rated program of all for several seasons. Crooning mc Rudy Vallée always managed to perform three or four songs during the course of the hour, while at the same time playing host to acts ranging from vaudeville comics to concert pianists. Standard Brands changed its sponsorship from Fleischmann's to Royal Gelatin in the summer of 1936. Vallée continued in this virtually identical show on NBC until 1939.

The Fleischmann Hour

The premiere show was October 24, 1929. The program would become a fixture on Thursdays from 8:00 to 9:00 p.m., running for 515 consecutive weeks until its final broadcast on September 28, 1939. Rudy himself

Graham McNamee

refused to take the customary summer vacation, and would miss only two shows in those 10 years: November 19, 1936, after his wife Fay died, and April 29, 1937 while on a ship heading for England where he would do two broadcasts from London. Many shows, including all those from the first three years, are believed to be lost. Graham McNamee was the announcer. By 1932, each hour saw scene(s) from recent films or notable plays, performed by distinguished actors, as noted. Some other significant guest stars, skits or songs are listed if known.

Kate Smith

1929:

10/24	Premiere
10/31	
11/7	
11/14	
11/21	
11/28	
12/5	
12/12	
12/19	
12/26	

1930:

1/2	Cliff Burwell, Lester Banker
1/9	Irene Bordoni
1/16	
1/23	Gladys Rice
1/30	Lily Damita, Phil Cook
2/6	Graham McNamee
2/13	Fanny Brice
2/20	Frances Maddux
2/27	Helen Morgan
3/6	

3/13	Olga Albani
3/20	Little Jack Little
3/27	National Cavaliers
4/3	Phil Cook
4/10	Marion Harris
4/17	Alan Waterous
4/24	Baby Rose Marie
5/1	National Cavaliers
5/8	Ruth Etting
5/15	Gitz-Rice and Five Canadian Mounties
5/22	The Keller Sisters and Lynch
5/29	Harry Braun
6/5	Frances Williams
6/12	Cavaliers Quartet
6/19	Rudy Wiedoeft
6/26	The Caroline Trio
7/3	Belle Baker
7/10	Frank Crumit
7/17	Ohman & Arden
7/24	
7/31	
8/7	
8/14	
8/21	
8/28	
9/4	Ruth Etting
9/11	
9/18	Little Jack Little
9/25	Rudy Wiedoeft

Otto Kruger

10/2	Cavaliers Quartet
10/9	The Caroline Trio
10/16	Molly Picon
10/23	Cavaliers Quartet
10/30	Kate Smith. "My Baby Just Cares for Me," "Just a Little Closer," "You'll Never Know, Sweetheart."
11/6	Goebel Reeves
11/13	Libby Holman
11/20	Eddie Peabody
11/27	The Brox Sisters
12/4	Jeanette MacDonald
12/11	Irene Bordoni
12/18	Ruth Etting
12/25	

1931:

1/1	
1/8	Kate Smith. "You're Driving Me Crazy"
1/15	Aileen Stanley
1/22	Helen Barr
1/29	Marion Harris
2/5	Eddie Cantor
2/12	Frances Langford
2/19	
2/26	Irene Bordoni
3/5	Harry Richman
3/12	Zelma O'Neal
3/19	Little Jack Little
3/26	Bernice Claire
4/2	Ray Perkins
4/9	Kate Smith. "Wabash Moon," "(Hi-Hi-Hi)

Just a Crazy Song," "By the River Ste. Marie"

4/16	Cavaliers Quartet
4/23	George Jessel
4/30	Helen Roland
5/7	Eddie Peabody
5/14	Cornelia Otis Skinner
5/21	Peggy Wood
5/28	Ruth Etting
6/4	Willie and Eugene Howard
6/11	The Rosamund Johnson Quartet
6/18	Julius Tannen
6/25	Frances Langford
7/2	The Man About Town Quartet
7/9	Ann Greenway
7/16	The Brox Sisters
7/23	Little Jack Little
7/30	Bernice Claire
8/6	Aileen Stanley
8/13	Ethel Waters
8/20	
8/27	Ray Perkins
9/3	Marion Harris
9/10	Walter O'Keefe
9/17	Ruth Etting
9/24	Joe Cook
10/1	Eddie Cantor
10/8	Borrah Minevitch
10/15	Tamara
10/22	Irene Bordoni

Joseph Schildkraut

10/29	Ginger Rogers
11/5	Belle Baker
11/12	Nancy Carroll
11/19	Sophie Tucker
11/26	Helen Morgan
12/3	Claire Madjette
12/10	Marion Harris
12/17	Fred and Adele Astaire
12/24	Ernestine Schumann-Heink
12/31	Mae Questel

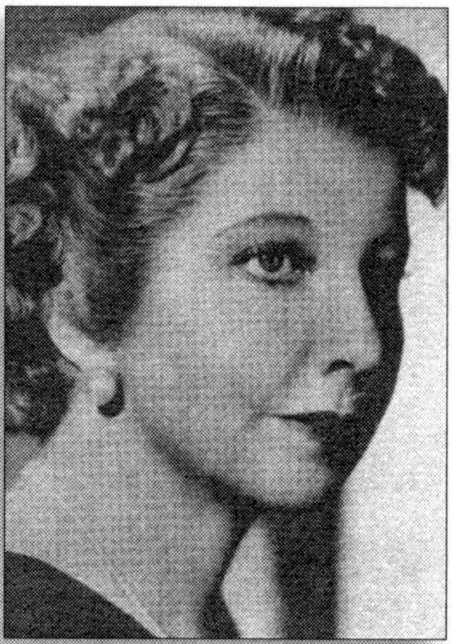

Helen Broderick

1932:

1/7	Lois Moran
1/14	Irene Bordoni
1/21	Beatrice Lillie
1/28	George Burns and Gracie Allen
2/4	
2/11	Lillian Roth
2/18	Bebe Daniels
2/25	Sylvia Froos
3/3	The Ponce Sisters
3/10	
3/17	The Mullins Sisters
3/24	Frances Williams
3/31	Sophie Tucker
4/7	The Foursome Quartet
4/14	Dorothy Dell
4/21	Irene Bordoni
4/28	
5/5	
5/12	

Claude Rains

5/19
5/26
6/2
6/9
6/16   Allen Waterous
6/23   Sophie Tucker
6/30   Holoua's Royal Hawaiians
7/7   Olsen and Johnson
7/14
7/21
7/28
8/4
8/11
8/18
8/25
9/1
9/8
9/15
9/22
9/29
10/6   Otis Skinner, Greta Keller
10/13   *Private Lives* Otto Kruger, Madge Kennedy
10/20   *Grand Hotel*
10/27   *Camille* Joseph Schildkraut, Beatrice Lillie
11/3   *Lulu Belle* Lenore Ulric, Phil Baker
11/10   *The Band Wagon* Helen Broderick,
        "Fascinating Rhythm," George Gershwin
11/17   *Street Scene* Marie Dressler
11/24   *Saturday's Children* Sylvia Field, Raymond Hackett
12/1   *Autumn Crocus* Francis Lederer
12/8

Fay Bainter

12/15	*Burlesque* Hal Skelly, Ethel Merman
12/22	*The Green Pastures*
12/29	*When Ladies Meet* George Jessel, Alice Faye

1933:

Montagu Love

1/5	*The Emperor Jones* Frank Wilson *H.M.S. Pinafore*
1/12	*Cyrano de Bergerac* Walter Hampden *Romeo and Juliet* Fanny Brice
1/19	*Cavalcade* Geoffrey Kerr, Victor Moore
1/26	*Twentieth Century* Eugenie Leontovich, Moffat Johnson, Lyda Roberti, Ray Bolger, Eugene and Willie Howard
2/2	A *Bill of Divorcement* Claude Rains, Mae West, Fred Astaire
2/9	*The Front Page* Osgood Perkins
2/16	*Romeo and Juliet* Jane Cowl, Jay C. Flippen
2/23	*Dr. Jekyll and Mr. Hyde* Conway Tearle
3/2	*The Valiant* Bert Lytell
3/9	*East Lynne* Edith Barrett, Helen Morgan
3/16	*Once in a Lifetime* Hugh O'Connell, Jean Dixon
3/23	*The Count of Monte Cristo* W.A. Brady, Robert Loraine
3/30	*Bittersweet* Peggy Wood
4/6	*For Services Rendered* Fay Bainter
4/13	*Anna Christie* Thomas Mitchell
4/20	*What Every Woman Knows* Helen Hayes, John Butler
4/27	*One Sunday Afternoon* Lloyd Nolan, Francesca Bruning
5/4	*There's Always Juliet* Margaret Sullavan, Tom Powers
5/11	*Death of Rasputin* Montagu Love, Jimmy Durante

5/18	*Trilby* William A. Brady, Irene Franklin
5/25	*Lady Tells All* Joan Blondell, Belle Baker
6/1	*A Marriage Has Been Arranged* Adolphe Menjou, K. Hepburn
6/8	Celebrity Night
6/15	*The 12 Pound Look* Ethel Barrymore, Walter O'Keefe
6/22	*Elizabeth the Queen* Judith Anderson
6/29	*A Comic Man* James Kirkwood, Max Baer, Doc Rockwell
7/6	*Death Takes a Holiday* Bert Lytell, Gilda Gray
7/13	*Divorcons* Grace George, Cliff Edwards
7/20	Paul Robeson, Aline Berry
7/27	*Private Lives* Robert Montgomery, Vera Allen
8/3	*Cyrano de Bergerac* Walter Hampden
8/10	*The Baby Carriage* Jennie Moscowitz, Walter O'Keefe
8/17	*Autumn Crocus* Dorothy Gish, Dino Nardi, Bobby Gilbert, Ukranian National Choir
8/24	*The Little Minister* Helen Hayes, John Griggs Joe Penner
8/31	*The Clod* Mary Morris, Lew Cody
9/7	*The Constant Lover* Geoffrey Kerr
9/14	Fay Bainter, Buster Keaton
9/21	*The Princess Marries the Page* Edith Barrett
9/28	Edgar Bergen & Charlie McCarthy
10/5	*The Coward* Guy Bates Post, Gladys Swarthout
10/12	*Murder at the Vanities* Bela Lugosi, Minnie Dupree
10/19	*Men in White* Margaret Barker, Alexander Kirkland
10/26	5th anniversary program. *The Green Pastures* Alice Faye, Deems Taylor, George Gershwin
11/2	*Berkeley Square* Conrad Nagel, Margalo Gilmore, Jack McClelland, Sarah and Sassafras
11/9	*The Love Nest* Jean Dixon, George Gershwin, Kitty Carlisle, Alice Faye

11/16   *Strictly Dishonorable* Margaret Sullavan,
          Alice Faye, Howard & Shelton, Cullins & Paterson
11/23   *Design for Living* Gary Cooper, Miriam Hopkins,
          Ernst Lubitsch, Adela Rogers St. Johns
11/30   *Spring in Autumn* Cesar Romero, Carol Stone
12/7   *Elizabeth the Queen* Judith Anderson
12/14   *Private Jones* James Cagney, Florence Desmond. The first
          Fleischmann broadcast from Hollywood.

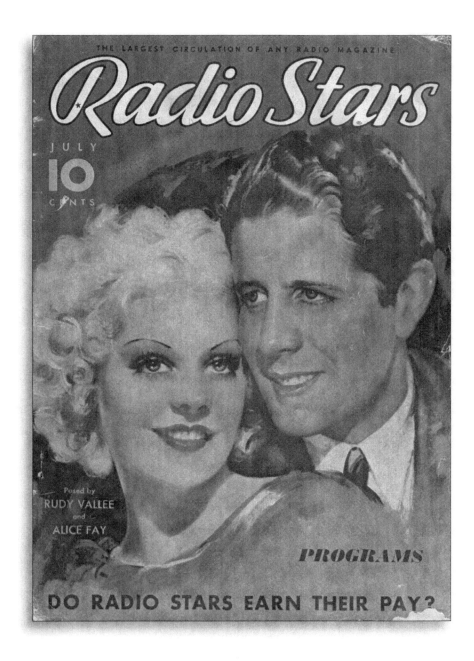

12/21 *The Curtain Rises* Ruby
       Keeler, Dick Powell
12/28 *The Last Roundup*
       William S. Hart

1934:

1/4   *Smilin' Through* Leslie Howard,
       Margaret Sullavan
1/11   *Blessed Event* Roger Pryor
1/18   *The Finger of God* Lionel Atwill
1/25   *Danger* Phillips Holmes,
       Thomas Holmes
2/1   *The Sorceress* Judith Anderson,
       Lenore Ulric
2/8   *The Choir Rehearsal* Helen
       Broderick, Helen Morgan,
       Joe Penner
2/15   *Anatol* Tallulah Bankhead
2/22   *Richard of Bordeaux* Dennis King,
       Margaret Vines
3/1   *Wealth and Wisdom*
       Colleen Moore, Joe Frisco
3/8   *A Cup of Coffee* Eddie Craven,
       Dorothy Parker
3/15   *Dodsworth* Walter Huston,
       Fay Bainter
3/22   *She Loves Me Not* John Beal,
       Florence Rice
3/29   Robert Montgomery
4/5   *The Man Who Came Through the
       Window* Joe Cook, Ilomay Bailey,
       Lee Sims

John Beal

Miriam Hopkins

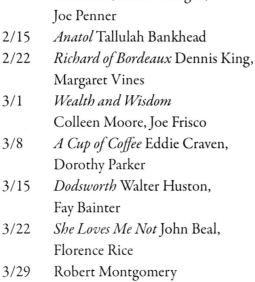

Robert Montgomery

4/12	*Three Who Found Death* Alice Faye
4/19	*Let Us Be Gay* Gloria Swanson (radio debut), Tom Powers, The Radio Aces
4/26	*The Queen's Husband* Roland Young
5/3	*Yellow Jack* James Stewart, Cab Calloway
5/10	*The Master of the Revels* Henry Hull, George Jessel
5/17	*The Other Place* Claude Rains, A.E. Matthews
5/24	*The Sire de Maletroit's Door* Melvyn Douglas, Helen Chandler
5/31	*Mary Stuart* Judith Anderson, Margaret Anglin
6/7	*The Valiant* Walter Huston, Alice Faye
6/14	*The Love Nest* Margaret Sullavan
6/21	*Spring Song* Richard Barthelmess
6/28	*Invitation to a Murder* Humphrey Bogart, Gale Page
7/5	Beatrice Lillie
7/12	*A Minuet* George Gaul, Frieda Inescort
7/19	*Phipps* Roland Young, Jimmy Savo
7/26	*What They Think* Ethel Barrymore Colt, Beatrice Lillie
8/2	*Cocktails for Two* Dorothy Stone, Stuart & Lash, Charles Collins, Borrah Minevitch
8/9	*Nurse's Day Out* Cornelia Otis Skinner, Robert Armstrong, Saxon Sisters, Milton Berle
8/16	*Hotel Porch* Cornelia Otis Skinner, Peggy Flynn, The Yacht Club Boys
8/23	*Adventures of Casper Milquetoast* Mr. & Mrs. Ernest Truex, Lillian Carmen, Lou Holtz, Cross & Dunn
8/30	*Crossed Roads* Elsie Mae Gordon, Jeanne Aubert, Chic Sale, Val & Ernie Stanton
9/6	*The Witch* Ilka Chase, Ruth Easton, Grace Moore
9/13	*The Love Nest* Wynne Gibson, Virginia Hale, Blossom Seeley, Benny Fields

RV with comedian Chic Sale and the Harry Jackson Orchestra

9/20   *Wednesday's Child* Frank Thomas

9/27   *Abraham Lincoln* Walter Huston

10/4   *The Happy Raven* Fanny Brice, Benny Krueger

10/11   *Death Takes a Holiday* Boris Karloff, The Shaw Group

10/18   *Long Live the King* Edward Everett Horton

10/25   *Four Walls* James Cagney

11/1   *Christmas* Barbara Stanwyck, Gale Gordon

11/8   A *Marriage Has Been Arranged* Ricardo Cortez

11/15   *Clear All Wires* Warren William, Helen Morgan

11/22   *Of Human Bondage* Bette Davis

11/29   *The Seven Ages of Parenthood* Bert Lahr, The Dirons

12/6   *The Monkey's Paw* Walter Huston, Helene Costello

Three of the biggest names in show business,
1935: Dick Powell, Rudy Vallée, Al Jolson

12/13   *The Farmer Takes a Wife* Henry Fonda, June Walker, Buck
      & Bubbles, Cole Porter, William S. Hart, Beatrice Lillie
12/20   Ben Lyon, Bebe Daniels, Lewis & Doty,
      Val & Ernie Stanton
12/27   *Alexander's Horse* Cornelia Otis Skinner, Blossom Seeley,
      Benny Fields, King Lavinsky, Tom Howard & George
      Shelton, The Stewart Sisters

1935:

1/3   *Valley Forge* Philip
      Merivale, Stanley Ridges,
      Harry Green, Juano
      Hernandez, Harold Elliot,
      George Stone
1/10   *Napoleon's Barber* Walter
      Connolly, Libby Holman,
      Johnny Burke,
      Yacht Club Boys

Basil Rathbone

1/17   *Accent on Youth* Constance
      Cummings
1/24   *Cyrano de Bergerac* Walter Hampden
1/31   *David Copperfield* Edmund Gwenn, Freddie Bartholomew
2/7   *The School for Scandal* Ethel Barrymore
2/14   *A Minuet* Leslie Howard, Merle Oberon
2/21   *Tobacco Road* Sam Byrd, Olga Baclanova
2/28   *Paolo and Francesca* Basil Rathbone
3/7   *Long Live the King* Frank Morgan
3/14   *Robert Emmett*, Dennis King, Victor Moore,
      Tom Howard & George Shelton
3/21   *Noah* Pierre Fresnay, Tom Howard & George Shelton,
      Earl Hines, Goode Sisters

3/28   *Saturday's Children* Roger Pryor, Peggy Conklin,
        Noah Beery, Henrietta Schuman

4/4   *The Tell-Tale Heart* Claude
        Rains, The Duncan Sisters,
        Ella Logan, Tom Howard
        & George Shelton

4/11   *Awake and Sing* Clifford
        Odets

4/18   *The Vinegar Tree* Mary
        Boland, Walter Connolly

4/25   *The Life Line* Judith
        Anderson, Ann Sothern

5/2   *Once in a Lifetime* Aline
        MacMahon, Lois Revel

May Robson

5/9   *The Firebrand* Fay Wray

5/16   *Dear Brutus* Leslie
        Howard, Leslie Ruth
        Howard

5/23   *Twentieth Century* John
        Barrymore

5/30   *The Three Musketeers* Gene
        Raymond

6/6   *Dream of the Marching
        Men* Anna Sten

6/13   *Last Mile* Lyle Talbot,
        Buddy Baer

6/20   *A Night's Work* May
        Robson, Eve Arden

Frank Morgan

6/27   *Dear Brutus* Leslie
        Howard, Leslie Ruth
        Howard, Henry Armetta, Joe Louis, Sigmund Spaeth

7/4   *Becky Sharp* Helen Hayes

7/11   *The Jest of Hahalaba* Clive
Brook, Anna May Wong,
Bob Burns

7/18   *The Third Angle* Gladys
George, Roy Smeck

7/25   *Elizabeth the Queen* Elissa
Landi

8/1   *Peg o' My Heart* Laurette
Taylor

8/8   *The Drunkard* Melvin
Purvis

8/15   *The Button* Henry Hull

8/22   *The Crusades* Henry Wilcoxon, Beatrice Lillie,
C.B. DeMille

8/29   The Dionne Quintuplets, Dr. Allan Dafoe

9/5   Bill Robinson, Robert Ripley

9/12   *Mr. Antonio* Leo Carrillo

9/19   *Blessed Event* Lee Tracy

9/26   *The Prince Chap* George
Brent, Lionel Atwill

10/3   *Mutiny on the Bounty*
Franchot Tone, Reginald
Gardiner

10/10   *Paths of Glory* Edward G.
Robinson

10/17   *Remember the Day*
Francesca Bruning
Todd Duncan

10/24   *Mary of Scotland* Gladys
Cooper, Lucienne Boyer,

Leo Carrillo

Mary Boland

Philip Merivale, Joseph
Levine, Stepin Fetchit

10/31   *Three Cornered Room*
Mary Boland, The Stewart
Sisters, Will Aubrey,
Josephine Baker

11/7   *The Lake* Miriam
Hopkins, Robert
Wildhock, Doris Weston,
Eddie Stanley

11/14   *The Other Place* Colin
Clive, Lew Lehr, James
Hilton, Evelyn Case,
Herbert Kingsley, Willie
& Eugene Howard, Leo G. Carroll

Franchot Tone

11/21   *Winterset* Burgess Meredith, Margo

11/28   *I Live My Life* Brian Aherne, Don Cossack Choir

12/5   *Clear All Wires* Pat O'Brien

12/12   *A Kiss for Cinderella* Jean Arthur

12/19   *Church Mouse* Una Merkel, Conrad Nagel, *May Wine*
Leo G. Carroll, Major Edward Bowes, Vera Van,
Sigmund Romberg

12/26   *Captain Blood* Errol Flynn

1936:

1/2   "How to Make the Most of 1936" Dr. Walter Pitkin

1/9   *St. Louis Blues* Frank Fay

1/16   *To Die With a Smile* Joseph Schildkraut, Lupé Velez

1/23   *Pursuit of Happiness* Paul Lukas, Peggy Conklin

1/30   *The Finger of God* Edward G. Robinson

2/6   *The Bells* Boris Karloff

EXCLUSIVE!! BOAKE CARTER REVEALS IMPORTANT UNPUBLISHED FACTS ABOUT HAUPTMANN!

Radio Stars

MAY
10
CENTS

Rudy Vallee

Earl Christy

THE LARGEST CIRCULATION OF ANY RADIO MAGAZINE

2/13   *A Tale of Two Cities* Blanche Yurka
2/20   *Lacrymosa* Marjorie Rawlings, Horace Braham
2/27   *The Artist* Douglas Fairbanks, Jr., June Walker,
         Helen Keller, Fay Wray, Ozzie Nelson, Harriet Hilliard,
         A.A. Milne
3/5   *Rich Kid* Freddie Bartholomew
3/12   *Ethan Frome* Raymond Massey
3/19   *St. Louis Blues* Alexander Kirkland, Freddie Lightner
3/26   *The Londonderry Air* Brian Aherne
4/2   *Box Car* Billy Halop, Kay Thompson
4/9   *The Prince of Peace* Richard Barthelmess
4/16   *The Beloved Voice* Ruth Chatterton
4/23   *Awake and Sing* Stella Adler, Alexander Kirkland, Eddie
         Cantor, Stuff Smith & his Orchestra, Hank Ladd
4/30   *Two Men in a Boat* Cornelia Otis Skinner
5/7   *Creation of Dr. Mallaire* Peter Lorre, Jean Hersholt
5/14   *Daughter of Evil* Judith Anderson
5/21   *The Sap from Syracuse* Hugh O'Connell
5/28   *Call it a Day* Gladys Cooper
6/4   *The Other Road* Robert Taylor, Milton Berle
6/11   *The Button* Henry Hull
6/18   *There's Always Juliet* Margaret Sullavan
6/25   *Murder in the Cathedral* Harry Irvine, Bert Lahr
7/2   Lupé Velez
7/9   *Within the Law* Josephine Hutchinson, Jean Arthur
7/16   *The Green Pastures* Rex Ingram, Gregory Ratoff
7/23   Bert Lahr, tribute to George Gershwin
7/30   *The Would-Be Gentleman* Jimmy Savo

The Royal Gelatin Hour

8/6   *Belief* Ricardo Cortez, Luise Rainer

8/13   *The Salesman* Charles Butterworth, Ilka Chase

8/20   *Private Lives*

8/27   *Art of Conversation* Mary Boland

9/3   Boris Karloff

9/10   John Boles

9/17   *Miraculous Visitor* Leslie Howard

9/24   *The Witch* Tallulah Bankhead

10/1

10/8   *Night Must Fall* Emlyn Williams

10/15   *St. Helena* Maurice Evans

10/22   *The Clock Strikes* Leonard Hollister

10/29   Rosalind Russell, Walter Abel

11/5   *Prelude to Murder* Olivia de Havilland, Peter Lorre

11/12   *One Special for Doc* Henry Hull

1/19   *Feeds* Billy Halop, Graham McNamee (guest mc), John McCormack, Adelaide Klein, Herbert Mundin. For the first time, Rudy Vallée does not appear, due to Fay's death.

11/26   *Prince and Maiden* Francis Lederer

12/3   *The Red Peppers* Noel Coward, Gertrude Lawrence, Ed Wynn, Eddie Peabody, John Gunther

Walter Abel

Olivia de Havilland

Charles Butterworth

12/10 *Captain Jones* Spencer Tracy

12/17 *3 of Diamonds Bid* Shirley Booth, Douglass
Montgomery, Edgar Bergen & Charlie McCarthy
(network radio debut), Cornelia Otis Skinner,
Elsa Maxwell

12/24 *That Strange Man* Walter Hampden

12/31 *Thank You, Mr. Krauss* Joseph Downing, Beatrice Lillie

1937:

1/7 *The Women* Margalo Gillmore

1/14 *Escape* Pat O'Brien, Walter O'Keefe, Sheila Barrett,
Bergen & McCarthy

1/21 *The Noble Land* Roland Young, Charioteers,
Sydney Franklin, Bergen & McCarthy

1/28 *Michael and Mary* Brian Aherne, Edith Barrett, Charlie
Butterfield, Percy Grainger, Men of Gotham Quartet

2/4 *Confession* Paul Lukas, Isabel Jewell, Bernard Bierman,
Bergen & McCarthy

2/11 *High Tor* Burgess Meredith, Bergen & McCarthy,
Walter O'Keefe

2/18 *Curtain* Jean Arthur, Sara Allgood, Bergen & McCarthy

2/25 *Dr. Hans* Jean Hersholt, Jean Sablon, Bergen & McCarthy,
Hilaire Belloc

3/4 *A Bill of Divorcement* Judith Anderson, Walter Abel,
Bergen & McCarthy, Mary Jane Walsh

3/11 *Art of Organization* Mary Boland, Hamilton College
Choir, Marjorie Hillis

3/18 *The Turning Point* Henry Fonda, Sylvia Field, Judy Starr,
Walter O'Keefe, Bergen & McCarthy

3/25 *Shadow Play* Tyrone Power, Florence Desmond,
Muriel Kirkland, Bob Hope, Tony Sarg

4/1   *Having Wonderful Time* Katherine Locke, Jules Garfield [John Garfield], Ryan & Lee, The Swing Kids

4/8   *The Harp* Henry Hull, Frank Capra, Eddie Green, Bergen & McCarthy

Frank Capra

4/15   *The Volunteer* Richard Bennett, Lou Holtz, Joan Edwards, Bergen & McCarthy

4/22   *The Conjure Drum* Mr. & Mrs. Cedric Hardwicke, Wynn Murray, Bergen & McCarthy

4/29   *The Game of Chess* Claude Rains. Rudy missed this show (only his second) as he was on a ship heading for London where he would broadcast the next two shows.

5/6   *Love for Love* Charles Laughton, Elsa Lanchester, Will Fyffe, Binnie Hale, Stanley Holloway

Jean Arthur

5/13   *The Wrong Bus* Fernand Gravet, Florence Desmond, Will Fyffe, J.B. Priestley

5/20   *Abie's Irish Rose* Ethel Merman, Maurice Evans, Juano Hernandez, Walter O'Keefe

5/27   *Autumn Flower* Anna May Wong

6/3   *The Breaking Point*

6/10   *Decision* Burgess Meredith

6/17   *Advice to the Little Peyton Girl* Tallulah Bankhead, Joe Laurie, Jr., Fanny Brice, Hanley Stafford, Dorothy Parker

RUDY VALLEE

6/24	*The Lady Was Worried* Dennis King
7/1	*The Gift of the Gods* Claude Rains
7/8	*The Man Who Thought of Everything* Douglas Fairbanks, Jr.
7/15	*The New Yorkers* Fay Wray
7/22	*One-Way Ticket* Ricardo Cortez
7/29	*Hamlet* Eddie Green
8/5	Molly Picon, Tommy Riggs & Betty Lou (radio debut)
8/12	*Mrs. Clifford Receives* Miriam Hopkins
8/19	*A Quiet Settlement* Gene Lockhart
8/26	*Loyalty* Conway Tearle, Erin O'Brien-Moore
9/2	*Some Day*
9/9	*The Testing of Oliver Beane* Burgess Meredith
9/16	*Paolo and Francesca* Maurice Evans, Edith Barrett, The Stroud Twins, Willie Howard, Tommy Riggs & Betty Lou
9/23	*Women of the World* Conrad Nagel
9/30	*Where the Green Apples Grow* Jean Muir
10/7	*Mr. Jones Changes His Mind* Edward Arnold
10/14	*The Bank Account* Walter Connolly
10/21	Mary Boland
10/28	*Rich Kid* Billy Halop
11/4	*Journey Postponed* Walter Huston
11/11	*Resurrection* Boris Karloff, William S. Hart
11/18	Eric Blore, Mischa Auer, Hedda Hopper, Tommy Riggs & Betty Lou
11/25	*Lo, the Poor Indian* John Barrymore, Elaine Barry, Eddie Green, Tommy Riggs & Betty Lou
12/2	*Lover Who Lost* The Abbey Players, Kay Thompson, Lou Holtz, Tommy Riggs & Betty Lou
12/9	*Of Mice and Men* Broderick Crawford, Wallace Ford, Bill Robinson, Tommy Riggs & Betty Lou, Oliver Wakefield
12/16	*Golden Boy* Frances Farmer, Luther Adler

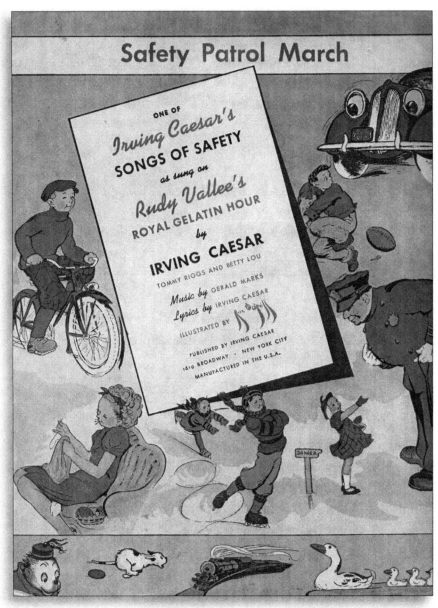

"Songs of Safety" Rose O'Neill, illustrator

Ralph Bellamy

12/23   *Ghost of Yankee Doodle*
       Ethel Barrymore, Dudley
       Digges, Hyman Kaplan,
       Oliver Wakefield

12/30   *Happy New Year, Pop*
       Frank Craven

1938:

1/6   *Time and the Conways*
       J.B. Priestley

1/13   *Dropped Stitches* Ralph
       Bellamy

1/20   *Picture Man* Peter Lorre

1/27   *Manhattan Latin*
       Humphrey Bogart, Glenda Farrell

2/3   *Cat with the Golden Eyes* Miriam Hopkins

2/10   *Mrs. Baffin* Mary Boland

2/17   *War Gardens* Fay Wray

2/24   *Lasses White and Honey
       Wiles* Andrea Leeds

3/3   *South of Wilshire*
       Betty Grable

3/10   *Begin at the End* Thomas
       Mitchell, Carmel Myers,
       Eric Linden, Tommy Riggs
       & Betty Lou, The
       Colorado Hillbillies

3/17   *Twilight Shore* Fay Bainter,
       Judith Anderson

3/24   *Roosty* William Harrigan, Maxine Sullivan, Colonel
       Stoopnagle, Tommy Riggs & Betty Lou

Andrea Leeds

3/31   *Prologue to Glory* Ann Rutledge
4/7   *White Cake* Ethel Barrymore, Tom Howard & George
        Shelton, Tommy Riggs & Betty Lou
4/14   *Master of the Revels* Maurice Evans, Edith Barrett,
        Fred Gradna, Tommy Riggs & Betty Lou, *Ever After*,
        Vincent Price
4/21   *For Future Reference* Arthur
        Byron, Tommy Riggs and
        Betty Lou
4/28   *What a Life!* Ezra Stone
5/5   *Dance Macabre* Boris
        Karloff, Tommy Riggs &
        Betty Lou, Colgate
        University Glee Club, East
        & Dumke
5/12   *The Circle* Jay C. Flippen,
        Grace George, Jimmy
        Lytell, Dennis Hoey,
        Tommy Riggs & Betty Lou

Peter Lorre

5/19   *Rendezvous with Tomorrow* Jane Cowl, Beatrice Fairfax,
        Rags Ragland, Tommy Riggs & Betty Lou
5/26   *No More Battles* Arthur Allen, The McNulty Family, Judy
        Canova, Tommy Riggs & Betty Lou
6/2   *The Shape of Darkness* Cedric Hardwicke
6/9   *Lamplighter of the Queer Street* Frank Craven,
        Franklin P. Adams, Rags Ragland, Tommy Riggs & Betty
        Lou, Joseph Holland
6/16   *Steelworker* Raymond Edward Johnson, Taylor Holmes,
        Lou Holtz, Tommy Riggs & Betty Lou
6/23   *'L' is for Love* Tallulah Bankhead, Franklin P. Adams,
        John Emery

6/30	*Two Bouquets* Patricia Morison, Alfred Drake, Eddie Green, Tommy Riggs & Betty Lou	
7/7	*He Caught a Tartar* Dennis King, Vera Zorina, Judy Canova, Slim & Slam	
7/14	*Cadenza* Ina Claire, Harold Vermilyea, Rags Ragland, Norman Rockwell, Jimmy Durante	
7/21	*The Doctor in Spite of Himself* Edward Everett Horton	
7/28	*Shadow Play* Gertrude Lawrence, Gabby Hartnett, Ezra Stone, Willie Howard	
8/4	*Test Flight* Paul Lukas	
8/11	*Henry Aldrich* Ezra Stone	
8/18	*Trilby* Walter Hampden, ZaSu Pitts	
8/25	*Whosis at the Dike* Frank Craven, Lillian Satanni, Ethel Merman, John Sebastian, Eric Blore	
9/1	*A Penny a Loaf* William A. Brady, Grace George, Bill Robinson, Elizabeth Haas	
9/8	*Meet the Folks* Hugh Herbert, Maurice Evans, Joe Cook, Franklin P. Adams	
9/15	*I Do* Brian Aherne	
9/22	*A Close Shave* Basil Rathbone	
9/29	*Design for Juliette* Onslow Stevens, Brian Aherne, Judy Canova, Sabu	
10/6	*Missouri Legend*	
10/13	*Stowaway* Freddie Bartholomew	
10/20	*Abe Lincoln in Illinois* Raymond Massey	
10/27	*Knickerbocker Holiday* Walter Huston	
11/3	*Little Dove* Lupé Velez	
11/10	*Mr. Pip* Walter Connolly	
11/17		
11/24	*Mrs. Weems and the Wanderlust* Billie Burke, Jane Warren, Four Squires	

12/1	*For Value Received* Billy Halop, Gladys George

12/1   *For Value Received* Billy Halop, Gladys George

12/8   *Professor Gossamer's Wings* Donald Meek, Elizabeth Paterson, Zane Grey, The King's Men

12/15   *The Rock* Broderick Crawford

12/22   *The Light* Richard Barthelmess

12/29   *Adventures of an Understanding Man* Guy Kibbee, *Five Minutes,* Billy Halop

Vera Zorina

1939:

1/5   *There's Always Joe Winters* Claude Rains

1/12   *The Best Policy* Franchot Tone

1/19   *Under the Skin* Guy Kibbee, C. Aubrey Smith

1/26   Hugh Herbert

2/2   *Entr'acte* Laurette Taylor

2/9   *Hometown* Walter Huston

2/16   *Henry IV* Maurice Evans

2/23   *The Gift* Judith Anderson

3/2   *Abe Lincoln in Illinois* Raymond Massey

3/9   *The Swan Song* Robert Morley

3/16

3/23   *Bayou Serenade* Margo

3/30   *The Eigerwund* Claude Rains

4/6   *Resurrection* Boris Karloff

4/13   *The Breaking Point* Kay Francis

4/20   *The Highwayman* Brian Aherne

Donald Meek

Billie Burke

4/27	*Ships That Pass in the Night* Gale Page
5/4	*W. Wilson by Poe* Herbert Marshall
5/11	Ann Harding
5/18	Anniversary Broadcast Lionel Barrymore
5/25	*Evening Song* Robert Morley
6/1	*The Boys from Syracuse* Paul Robeson
6/8	*Alias Capt. Battle* Fay Wray
6/15	*Joe, the Motorman* Rubinoff
6/22	Dorothy Lamour
6/29	May Robson
7/6	*Suppressed Desires* Constance Bennett
7/13	Bert Lahr
7/20	*The Still Alarm* Laurence Olivier
7/27	*Jenny Learns Quickly* Erin O'Brien-Moore
8/3	*Roses for Fifi* John Barrymore
8/10	Peter Lorre
8/17	*The Man in Possession* Bela Blau
8/24	Jimmy Durante
8/31	
9/7	*Card Tricks* Shirley Booth
9/14	*Café Casualty* Gertrude Lawrence
9/21	*Wedding Present* Leon Janney
9/28	Jimmy Durante

4. *The Rudy Vallée (Sealtest) Show*

Rudy Vallée's show in a 30-minute format ran on NBC from 1940-1943. Unlike his earlier shows, this was a comedy program, with a weekly sketch taking up most of the half-hour, though Vallée still managed to slip in a couple of songs per broadcast. The show's theme song was "Those Little Nothings," by Bobby Worth and Stanley Cowan. Singer Susan Miller was a semi-regular. The show often boasted interest-

ing stars, with John Barrymore appearing as a permanent guest. Ironically, the "Farewell Barrymore" skit set for the May 14, 1942 show would nearly be the Great Profile's last. He collapsed during rehearsal and died on May 29, 1942.

1940:

3/7	Premiere episode
3/14	through 8/8 (22 broadcasts)
8/15	"The Story of Robert Fulton." Mitzi Green, Colonel Stoopnagle
8/22	"The Story of the Hatfields and the McCoys." Walter O'Keefe, Dinah Shore
8/29	"The Story of Robert Burns." Peg LaCentra, Betty Garde
9/5	
9/12	"The Story of Robin Hood." Joe Penner, Keenan Wynn
9/19	

Producer Dick Mack surrounded by staff writers Paul Hennings, Charlie Isaacs, Jess Oppenheimer, Mannie Manheim (l. to r.)

9/26   "The Story of Diamond Jim Brady." Shirley Ross, Eddie Green

10/3   "The Story of Thomas Moore." Audrey Marsh, Betty Garde

10/10

10/17

10/24

10/31   Vote for the greater lover: "The Great Profile" or "The Vagabond Lover"?

11/7

11/14	"Rudy Vallée's Day in Hollywood." Maxie Rosenbloom
11/21	"Colossal Town." Vera Vague
11/28	"Don Juan Escort Bureau." Billie Burke, Lurene Tuttle
12/5	
12/12	
12/19	*Julius Caesar* Orson Welles
12/26	Billie Burke, Harold Peary, Sigrid Gurie

announcer **Bill Stulla**

1941:

1/2	Julietta Novis, Susan Miller, Joseph Lilly
1/9	"Rudy of the Mounties." Vera Vague, Lurene Tuttle
1/16	"The Horror Picture." Susan Miller, Orson Welles
1/23	
1/30	
2/6	
2/13	

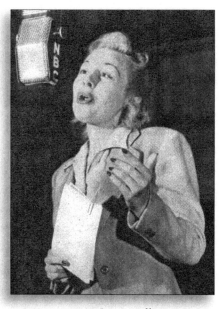

singer **Susan Miller**

2/20	
2/27	
3/6	
3/13	
3/20	
3/27	Groucho Marx
4/3	
4/10	
4/17	
4/24	
5/1	*Richard III* Lionel Barrymore
5/8	"What's What in Kilowatts?" Orson Welles
5/15	"The Ultraconservative Conservatory." Frank Fay, José Iturbi
5/22	
5/29	*Million Dollar Baby* Priscilla Lane
6/5	*Hamlet* Lionel Barrymore, Susan Miller
6/12	Marie Wilson, Edmund Lowe
6/19	Marjorie Rambeau, Phil Silvers
6/26	Mischa Auer, Mercedes McCambridge, Susan Miller
7/3	Bud Abbott, Lou Costello, The King's Men
7/10	Martha Raye
7/17	
7/24	
7/31	
8/7	"Boarding House." Edna May Oliver, Florence Gill (voice of "Clara Cluck") sings
8/14	"Barbecue." Susan Miller, Billy Gilbert, Verna Felton
8/21	"Barrymore & Barrymore Real Estate Company." Lionel Barrymore, The King's Men
8/28	through 12/25 (18 broadcasts)

At rehearsal (l. to r.) Dick Mack (producer), Mercedes McCambridge,
Mischa Auer, John Barrymore, RV, Susan Miller, Joe Parker (producer)

Shirley Temple

1942:

1/1 through 5/14 (20 broadcasts)

5/21 "Barrymore Investment Company." Joan Davis, Stu Erwin. Barrymore's final show before his death on May 29.

5/28

6/4

6/11

6/18

6/25

7/2

7/9

7/16

7/23

7/30

8/6

Gene Autry

8/13   "The Village Store." Joan Davis, Reginald Gardiner. Dick Mack reads Vallée's part, as he misses this show, due to his impending induction in the Coast Guard.

8/20   through 12/31 (20 broadcasts)

1943:

1/7   through 7/1 (26 broadcasts)

7/8   RV's final appearance

On July 8, 1943, Rudy left the show for active duty in the Coast

Guard, turning the program over to Joan Davis. She had been appearing with him semi-regularly for some months. Davis, along with Jack Haley, would continue virtually the same format under the name *The Sealtest Village Store.*

5. *Coast Guard Show* NBC 1943-1944

During his active duty, Rudy and the Coast Guard Band broadcast a series of 15-minute programs, transcribed at the NBC Hollywood studios. These were designed to inspire enlistments and encourage the buying of war bonds. He was discharged from the service in July 1944.

1943: (example):

10/28   "Coast Guard (Lt.) Rudy Vallée" Joan Davis

6. *Villa Vallée – The Drene Show* NBC 1944-1947

This half-hour variety show ran on Saturday evenings from 8:00 to 8:30 until November 4, 1944, then switching to Thursdays from 10:30 to 11:00 p.m. Sponsored by Drene Shampoo for the entire run, other regulars were Les Paul, Edith Gwynn and (starting in November 1944) Monty Woolley.

1944:

9/6   "Drene Preview Show" audition
9/9   Premiere show. Ingrid Bergman, Michael Chekhov
9/16   Ed Gardner, the Les Paul Trio, Loulie Jean Norman
9/20   "Preview Show"
9/23   "For Whom the Bells Toll." Benny Carter, Mantan Moreland, Doodles Weaver, Katina Paxinou
9/30   Martha Raye, Robert Maxwell
10/7   Joan Davis, Les Paul, Tudor Williams
10/14   "The Talk of the Town." Carmel Myers, Vera Vague, Cathy Lewis, Benny Carter, Mantan Moreland

10/21   "Brooklyn." William Bendix, Rosa Linda, Les Paul,
          Joan Barton
10/28
11/4   Doodles Weaver, Ethel Waters

11/9	"Commercials." Fred Allen, Shirley Temple, Janis Paige
11/16	Tallulah Bankhead, Billy Roy
11/23	"College Life." Lionel Stander, Betty Jane Greer
11/30	"Professor Woolley at Yale." Vivian Blaine
12/7	
12/14	Vivian Blaine
12/21	Betty Jane Greer
12/28	Marjorie Bayne

Monty Woolley

1945:

1/4	Anita O'Day
1/11	"Detective Story"
1/18	The Andrews Sisters
1/25	
2/1	Ed Gardner, Anita Boyer
2/8	Irene Ryan
2/15	Bud Abbott, Lou Costello
2/22	Irene Ryan
3/1	Irene Ryan
3/8	"The Rudy Vallée Story"
3/15	Irene Ryan
3/22	"Automobiles." Irene Ryan
3/29	Irene Ryan
4/5	The Barry Sisters, Irene Ryan
4/12	
4/19	Ralph Edwards, Sarah Berner, Irene Ryan

Joan Davis

NELSON EDDY Gives His Frankest Interview

Radio Guide

THE NATIONAL WEEKLY OF PRO

WEEK ENDING JUNE 13, 1936

10 CENTS

EXPLAINING
FIFI D'ORSAY

SCOOP!
What Freedom Cost
Rudy Vallee

4/26	Adolphe Menjou, Irene Ryan, The Barry Sisters
5/3	through 11/29 (31 broadcasts)
12/6	Billie Burke, Xavier Cugat Orchestra
12/13	Billie Burke, Xavier Cugat Orchestra
12/20	Ken Murray, Marie Wilson, Xavier Cugat Orchestra
12/27	Billie Burke, Xavier Cugat Orchestra

1946:

1/3	Gloria Blondell, Eddie Marr
1/10	Virginia Mayo, Gloria Blondell, Eddie Marr
1/17	Alan Ladd, Eddie Marr
1/24	Dizzy Gillespie, Jean Hersholt, Eddie Marr
1/31	Leo McCarey
2/7	
2/14	Joan Bennett
2/21	Celeste Holm
2/28	Edward Arnold
3/7	
3/14	Ella Logan
3/21	Patsy Moran
3/28	Robert Alda, Ella Logan
4/4	Robert Alda, Ella Logan
4/11	Constance Bennett, Patsy Moran
4/18	Basil Rathbone, Patsy Moran
4/25	Basil Rathbone
5/2	Lynn Bari
5/9	Audrey Totter
5/16	Veronica Lake
5/23	Marie McDonald, Dinah Shore, Jack Smith
5/30	Dinah Shore, Jack Smith
6/6	Gracie Fields, Dinah Shore, Jack Smith

6/13   Dinah Shore, Jack
Smith
    6/20   Peter Lorre, Dinah
            Shore, Jack Smith
    6/27   Dinah Shore, Jack
            Smith

Dinah Shore

7. **Johnny Presents the *Rudy***
Vallée Show (*The Philip Morris*
Show)

Vallée's final NBC show ran
from September 10, 1946 to March
4, 1947 on Tuesdays from 8:00-8:30
p.m.; being sponsored for the entire run of 26 broadcasts by Philip Morris Cigarettes.

1946:
    9/10   Harold Peary
    9/17   Tommy Dorsey
    9/24   Eve Arden, Charles
            Trenet
    10/1
    10/8
    10/15
    10/22
    10/29   William Bendix
    11/5
    11/12
    11/19   Yvonne Pershing,
            Benny Krueger and his
            Orchestra

"Smiling" Jack Smith

11/26
12/3
12/10
12/17
12/24
12/31   Margaret Whiting,
        Ken Gard, Bill Stern

Eve Arden

1947:
1/7   *Two Years Before the Mast*
      Alan Young, Doris Day
1/14 *Mrs. Weems and the
      Wanderlust* Mildred &
      Jimmy Mulcay, Billie Burke,
      Ken Gard
1/21 George Murphy, Ruth Etting
1/28 George Murphy, Ruth Etting, Mildred & Jimmy Mulcay
2/4   "In a Pugilistic Way." Walter O'Keefe, Ruth Etting, The
      Tune Toppers
2/11 Margo, Eddie Albert, Pat Patrick, Jane Harvey
2/18 *The Button* Walter O'Keefe, Kirk Douglas, Mildred &
      Jimmy Mulcay. Live broadcast from the Last Frontier
      Hotel in Las Vegas
2/25 The Wesson Brothers, Jane Harvey, The Tune Toppers.
      Live broadcast from the Last Frontier Hotel in Las Vegas
3/4   "The Powder Room." Barbara Luddy, Cathy Lewis, Lurene
      Tuttle, Dave Barry, Jane Harvey

8. *Rudy Vallée Show*

Back where he began some 20+ years before, on a local NYC show, starting in February 1950, Rudy Vallée could be found playing records and talking for WOR/Yankee Network. Some of the sponsors of the

30-minute show included Miller Beer, Super Suds, Lydia Pinkham, and Bon Ami.

1950:   (one example):

    4/27   Vic Roby (announcer). RV discusses two competing color television systems, anecdotes about Paul Lukas; records include "Sunshine Cake."

Band Remotes

During the 1930s Rudy Vallée and His Connecticut Yankees were heard regularly in remote broadcasts from various clubs — the Hotel Astor, French Casino, Hollywood Restaurant, Coconut Grove, Arcadia Restaurant, Manhattan Beach and others. Following is a sample of some of these performances.

1936:

    6/6   From the Hotel Astor roof, Connie Miles, Judy Starr, Three Graces, The Gentlemen Songsters. NBC (30 min.)

    6/8   From the Hotel Astor roof, The Stewart Sisters. NBC (30 min.)

    6/18   Carol Gould, Al Lewis. NBC (30 min.)

    6/25   Carol Gould, Sammy Cahn, Saul Chaplin. NBC (30 min.)

1937:

    5/29   From the Hotel Astor roof, The Swing Kids, Willie Versachi. NBC

    6/1   Judy Starr. NBC (30 min.)

    6/5   Judy Starr. NBC (30 min.)

    6/8   Judy Starr. NBC (30 min.)

    6/15   Pat Ellington, The Swing Kids, The Stewart Sisters. NBC (30 min.)

6/19   From the Hotel Astor roof, Judy Starr, The Swing Kids.
        WJZ (15 min.)

6/26   From the Hotel Astor roof, Judy Starr, The Swing Kids,
        Willie Versachi, Cy Baker. (15 min.)

6/29   From the Hotel Astor roof, Pat Ellington, The Gentlemen
        Songsters. (15 min.)

7/3   From the Hotel Astor roof, Pat Ellington, Cy Baker.
        NBC (15 min.)

1938:

5/28   From the Hotel Astor roof, Dorothy Appelby.
        WEAF (15 min.)

5/31   From the Hotel Astor roof, Billy Hill. NBC (30 min.)

6/7   From the Hotel Astor roof, Carol Gould, Mabel Wayne,
        The Gentlemen Songsters. WJZ (15 min.)

6/11   From the Hotel Astor roof, Carol Gould.
        WEAF (15 min.)

6/14   From the Hotel Astor roof, Larry Clinton. WJZ (15 min.)

1939:

5/16   From the Hotel Astor roof, Judy Starr. (15 min.)

5/23   From the Hotel Astor roof, Lola London, The Gentlemen
        Songsters. (15 min.)

1946:

Date?   Opening night from the Club Moderne; Ken Murray
        (host), Marie Wilson, Gene Austin and other friends
        perform from Murray's *Blackouts* show. KGER Long
        Beach, California

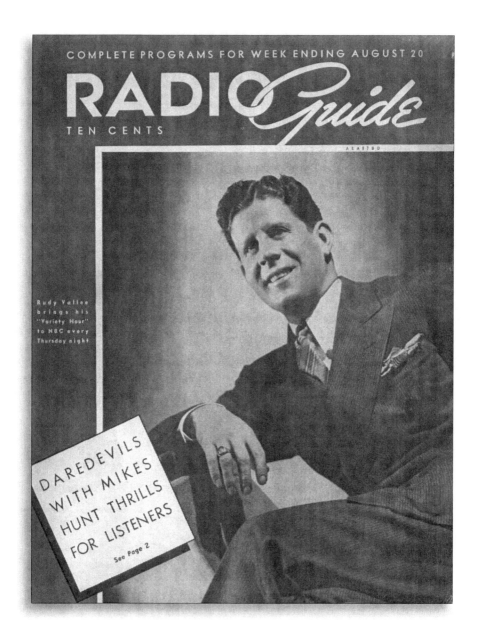

Guest Radio appearances:

Busy as he was with his own weekly shows, Rudy Vallée managed to appear on numerous other radio programs. Following is a sampling of many of these guest appearances.

1935:

1/16   *Radio City Matinee* Hazel Glenn, The Sisters of the Skillet, The Stewart Sisters. NBC (1 hr.)

12/7   *NBC Hollywood Studio Opening* Ruth Etting, Al Jolson, Irene Rich, Bing Crosby, Jack Benny, Mary Livingstone, James Melton, Ben Bernie, Paul Whiteman, Jimmy Durante, May Robson, Grantland Rice. NBC (150 min.)

Ruth Etting

1936:

2/23   *The Magic Key*
Love on a Bet Gene Raymond, Sidney Fox. NBC (1 hr.) #22

1937:

10/3   *Chase & Sanborn Hour* Edgar Bergen & Charlie McCarthy, Sally Eilers, Nelson Eddy, Dorothy Lamour. Rudy Vallée (guest mc for Don Ameche). NBC (1 hr.) #22

1938:

4/25   *The Eddie Cantor Show* Rudy Vallée (host for an ill
Cantor), Bert Gordon, Jane Froman. CBS (30 min.) #5
for Camel

8/3   "Tribute to Irving Berlin." Al Jolson (mc), Irving Berlin
(special guest), Walter Winchell, Eddie Cantor, Sophie
Tucker, Ben Bernie, Lew Lehr, The Brox Sisters, Belle
Baker, Connie Boswell, Ethel Merman, John Steele,
Louella Parsons, Darryl F. Zanuck, Alice Faye, Tyrone
Power, Jack Haley, Ted Husing, Orchestras of Tommy
Dorsey, Guy Lombardo, Paul Whiteman. CBS (75 min.)

Irving Berlin

1939:

4/9   *Gulf Screen Guild Theater* "Variety Review 5" Mickey
       Rooney, Joan Bennett, Rosemary Lane, The King's Men,
       George Murphy. CBS (30 min.) #14

6/26   *The Magic Key* "Second Fiddle," Irving Berlin, Tyrone
       Power, Sonja Henie, Tommy Dorsey & his Orchestra,
       Darryl F. Zanuck. NBC (1 hr.) #196

11/12 *Chase & Sanborn Hour* Edgar Bergen & Charlie
       McCarthy, Jean Arthur. Rudy Vallée (guest mc for Don
       Ameche for the next five shows). NBC (1 hr.) #132

11/19 *Chase & Sanborn Hour* Edgar Bergen & Charlie
       McCarthy, John Garfield. NBC (1 hr.) #133

11/26 *Chase & Sanborn Hour* Edgar Bergen & Charlie
       McCarthy, Loretta Young. NBC (1 hr.) #134

12/3   *Chase & Sanborn Hour* Edgar Bergen & Charlie
       McCarthy, Maureen O'Hara, Arthur Treacher.
       NBC (1 hr.) #135

12/10 *Chase & Sanborn Hour* Edgar Bergen & Charlie
       McCarthy, Lansing Hatfield. NBC (1 hr.) #136 Christmas
       broadcast from hospital

1940:

2/26   *Lux Radio Theatre* "Swing High, Swing Low." RV (Skid
       Johnson), Virginia Bruce (Maggie King), Una Merkel
       (Ella), Roscoe Karns (Harry), Cecil B. DeMille (host),
       Melville Ruick (announcer). Songs: "Adios," "I Didn't
       Know What Time it Was," "All the Things You Are."
       CBS (1 hr.) #252.

3/1   "Rudy Vallee Alumni Reunion Banquet." Eddie Cantor
       (toastmaster), George Burns, Gracie Allen, Ken Murray,
       Bob Burns, Frances Langford. (30 min.)

8/23   *Command Performance.* "The Life Story of Rudy Wiedoeft." Rudy Vallée tells the story of his mentor. (30 min.)

Frances Langford

1941:

1/22   *The Eddie Cantor Show* (*It's Time to Smile*) Eddie Cantor, Harry Von Zell, Dinah Shore. NBC (30 min.) #17 for Sal Hepatica.

12/14   *We Hold These Truths!* Norman Corwin (by), Edward Arnold, Walter Brennan, Bob Burns, Walter Huston, Marjorie Main, Edward G. Robinson, Corporal James Stewart, Orson Welles. Music by Bernard Herrmann. CBS, NBC, Mutual (1 hr.)

Deanna Durbin

1942:

5/18   *Command Performance* George Raft (mc), Brenda & Cobina, Deanna Durbin, Bea

	Benaderet, Meade "Lux" Lewis, Dinah Shore, The Sportsmen Quartet. AFRS (30 min.) #14
10/3	"Hollywood Canteen Opening." Bette Davis, Eddie Cantor, Abbott & Costello, Dinah Shore, Betty Hutton, Ginny Simms. NBC (30 min.)
10/14	*The Eddie Cantor Show* (*It's Time to Smile*) Eddie Cantor, Harry Von Zell, Dinah Shore, Hattie McDaniel, Bert Gordon. NBC (30 min.) #84 for Sal Hepatica.
Date?	*Mail Call* (#104) "Way, Way Down East." Fred Allen, Frank Sinatra, Gloria DeHaven, Mary Livingstone. AFRS (30 min.)
Dates?	*Treasury Song Parade* Each program contains a public service announcement for war bonds and a song by Rudy Vallée. Treasury Department Syndication (3.5 min. each) #365 "Semper Paratus" #366 "The Fleet's in Port Again" #367 "The Red, White and Blue" #368 "Last Roundup" #369 "Sing a Tropical Song" #370 "I Left My Sugar in Salt Lake City"
Dates?	*Treasury Star Parade* Treasury Department Syndication (15 min.) #63 "I Carry the Mail." Tribute to mailmen #65 "Blues in the Night." WWI songs medley #67 "Where To?" Tribute to cab-drivers

1943:

1/27	*The Eddie Cantor Show* (*It's Time to Smile*) Eddie Cantor, Harry Von Zell, Dinah Shore, Bert Gordon, Hattie McDaniel, Betty Hutton (guest). NBC (30 min.) #99 for Sal Hepatica

3/15   *The Lady Esther Screen Guild Theater The Palm Beach Story.* Claudette Colbert, Randolph Scott. CBS (30 min.) #135 for Lady Esther

4/10   *Open House Party.* Paul Whiteman honored for being named Director of Music for the Blue network. Paul Whiteman, Gracie Allen, Morton Downey, Mildred Bailey, Walter Damrosch, Chester Lauck, Norris Goff, Gracie Fields, Johnny Mercer, Orchestras of Jimmy Dorsey, Tommy Dorsey, Henry Busse, Matty Matlock. Blue Network (90 min.)

6/18   *Comedy Caravan* "Vallée Varieties." Victor Borge, Dorothy Lamour, The King Sisters. NBC (30 min.)

11/25   *The Lifebuoy Show* Bob Burns, Spike Jones and the City Slickers, The Nilsson Twins. RV loses his place in the script. NBC (30 min.)

Date?   *Uncle Sam Presents* Jimmy Grier (conductor), The Eleventh Naval District Coast Guard Band. RV makes an extraordinarily bad straight-man! O.W.I. Syndication (16 min.) #31

Spike Jones

Date?   *Uncle Sam Presents* RV (director), The Eleventh Naval District Coast Guard Band, Hoagy Carmichael. An uninter-

rupted medley of Carmichael's songs. O.W.I.
Syndication (16 min.) #32

1944:

6/16   *Your All-Time Hit Parade* Harry Von Zell (announcer),
Bonnie Lou Williams, The Sentimentalists, Bob Allen. RV
just finished his Coast Guard active service, sings "Deep
Night." NBC (30 min.)

9/9   *Johnny Mercer's Music Shop* Johnny Mercer, The Pied
Pipers, June Hutton, Jo Stafford, Paul Weston and His
Orchestra. NBC (15 min.) #44

9/15   *Duffy's Tavern* Ed Gardner. NBC (30 min.) #59

12/17   *Chase & Sanborn Program* Edgar Bergen & Charlie
McCarthy. NBC (30 min.)

Date?   *Sound Off.* Record of RV's "San Fernando Valley" opens
the show. AFRS (15 min.) #374

1945:

1/3   *The Frank Sinatra Show* Frank Sinatra, Bill Goodwin
(announcer), Axel Stordahl and His Orchestra, Eileen
Barton, The Ken Lane Singers. CBS (30 min.)

1/14   *The Andrews Sisters* Andrews Sisters, Gabby Hayes. CBS
(30 min.) #3

2/15   *The Abbott and Costello Show* "Jack and the Beanstalk."
Bud Abbott, Lou Costello, Connie Haines.
NBC (30 min.)

10/14   *Request Performance* "Huckleberry Finn." Jimmy Lydon,
Diana Lynn, Frank Morgan, Hoagy Carmichael. CBS
(30 min.) #2

10/27   "A Salute to the Fleet." Henry Fonda, Robert Taylor,
Frances Langford, John Charles Thomas. NBC (30 min.)

The Andrews Sisters

11/1   *Birdseye Open House* Dinah Shore (host), Frank Nelson,
         Harry Von Zell, The Four Hits. RV recalls days at Yale.
         NBC (30 min.)
12/26   *The Andrews Sisters* CBS (30 min.) #42

1946:

2/24   *Request Performance* "One for the Money." Jerry Colonna, Edward Arnold, Cass Daley. CBS (30 min.) #21

3/24   *Radio Hall of Fame* "Sorry, Wrong Number." (RV forgets his lines during the drama) Agnes Moorehead, Martha Tilton. ABC (30 min.)

7/21   *The Tommy Dorsey Show* Tommy Dorsey and His Orchestra, Wendell Niles (announcer), Stuart Foster, Ziggy Elman, The Sentimentalists, Duet: Tommy (trombone) and Rudy (sax). NBC (30 min.)

Date?   *Moondial* Eddie Gallaher interviews RV and plays a number of his most well-known recordings. WTOP, Washington, D.C. (25 min.)

Date?   "The True Glory of Thanksgiving." RV (introducer), plea for assistance from the Greek War Relief Fund. Syndicated (15 min.)

Date?   *Show Stoppers* "Rudy Vallée." Knox Manning (host), RV tells how he became a star and "stopped the show" and, of course, sings. Sponsored by Koret of California, Textile Broadcasts Inc. Syndication (15 min.) #15

1947:

1/24   *Bill Stern's Colgate Sports Newsreel* NBC (15 min.) #376

5/25   *The Fred Allen Show* "Gimmick with a Microphone." Fred Allen, Portland Hoffa, Kenny Delmar, Parker Fennelly, Minerva Pious, Alan Reed. NBC (30 min.) #72 for Tenderleaf Tea.

6/18   *Duffy's Tavern* Ed Gardner. NBC (30 min.)

9/9   *Command Performance* Rudy Vallée (mc), Dorothy Patrick, Lolita Castegnaro, June Foray, Reginald Gardiner, Michel Perriere and the AFRS Orchestra. AFRS (30 min.) #292

1948:

11/29   *The Railroad Hour* "New Moon." Gordon MacRae (host/star), Nadine Conner. ABC (45 min.) #9

1949:

1/30   *The Fred Allen Show* "Howdy Doody." Fred Allen, Portland Hoffa, Kenny Delmar, Parker Fennelly, Minerva Pious, Alan Reed. NBC (30 min.) #44 for Ford Motor Company.

2/25   *Bill Stern's Colgate Sports Newsreel* Bill Stern, Mrs. John McGraw on 15th anniversary of husband's death. NBC (15 min.) #487

Fred Allen

4/20   *Philco Radio Time* "A Visit to Rudy Vallée." Bing Crosby, Walter O'Keefe, John Scott Trotter, The Rhythmaires. ABC (30 min.)

4/28   *The Sealtest Variety Theater* (*The Dorothy Lamour Show*) "Betting on a Horse Race." Dorothy Lamour, Eddie Bracken, Frank Nelson, Alan Reed (guest). NBC (30 min.) #31

6/16   *The Burns and Allen Show* (*Maxwell House Coffee Time*) "Teenage Girl in Love with Rudy Vallée." George Burns, Gracie Allen, Richard Crenna, Marylee Robb. NBC (30 min.) #38

George Burns and
Gracie Allen

1951

1/28   *The Big Show* Tallulah Bankhead (host), Danny Kaye, Gary
       Cooper, Ray Bolger, Maxie Rosenbloom, Julie Wilson,
       Ernest Hemingway, The Delta Rhythm Boys. NBC
       (90 min.) #13

4/8   *The Big Show* Tallulah Bankhead (host), Fred Allen, Jimmy
       Durante, Vivian Blaine, Jane Morgan. NBC (90 min.) #23

1952:

1/11   *The Toast of the Town* Harry Richman, George M. Cohan,
       Jr., Jack Buchanan, Georgie Price and son Peter.
       CBS (30 min.)

Date?   *Guest Star Time* RV: "Something to Remember You By."
       Sister Elizabeth Kenny Foundation fund appeal.
       Syndication (15 min.) #KBR-11

1954:

6/20   *The Edgar Bergen Show with Charlie McCarthy.* Nelson Eddy & Charlie play excerpts from previous broadcasts. Jimmy Stewart, Don Ameche, Marilyn Monroe, Lionel Barrymore. CBS (30 min) last show of 16th season.

1955:

2/27   *Kraft Music Hall* Rudy Vallée (host), Gwen Verdon, Steve Allen, Julie Andrews, Eddie Condon. NBC (1 hr.)

3/13   *Kraft Music Hall* Rudy Vallée (host), Carmen MacRae, Jack E. Leonard, Earl Wilson. NBC (1 hr.)

3/20   *Kraft Music Hall* Rudy Vallée (host), Benny Goodman, Shirl Conway, Joey Adams, Greta Keller. NBC (1 hr.)

4/3   *Kraft Music Hall* Rudy Vallée (host), Mitch Miller, Agnes de Mille, Kay Ballard. NBC (1 hr.)

1956:

5/6   *The New Edgar Bergen Hour* 20th anniversary of Bergen & McCarthy on radio, excerpts from previous shows' highlights include: Nelson Eddy, John Barrymore, Marilyn Monroe, James Stewart. (1 hr.)

7/4   *Recollections at 30* (Excerpts from some of NBC's greatest shows, celebrating its 30th year in broadcasting.) Lum & Abner, Frances Langford, Clark & McCullough (radio debut), Al Jolson, RV on *The Fleischmann Hour* 7/4/35. NBC (25 min.) #3

7/11   *Recollections at 30* Bob Burns, Bing Crosby, Jesse Owens, Ralph Edwards, Tom Howard & George Shelton on *The Fleischmann Hour* 7/4/35. NBC (25 min.) #4

8/15   *Recollections at 30* Deanna Durbin, Eddie Cantor, Father Coughlin, Bebe Daniels, Ben Lyon. NBC (25 min.) #9

11/14   *Recollections at 30* Judy Garland, John McCormack, Edgar Bergen & Charlie McCarthy (debut) on *The Fleischmann Hour* 12/17/1936. NBC (25 min.) #21

11/21   *Recollections at 30* Jack Benny, Fred Allen, Helen Kane, Dorothy Lamour, Fred MacMurray. RV, Gloria Grafton & Richard Rodgers sing songs from *Jumbo* on *The Fleischmann Hour,* 1935. NBC (25 min.) #22

12/12   *Recollections at 30* Lanny Ross, Floyd Gibbons, Carmen Miranda, Art Tatum, John Barrymore, Jack Pearl on *The Fleischmann Hour.* NBC (25 min.) #25

12/19   *Recollections at 30* Cliff Edwards, Gloria Swanson, Walter Huston sings "September Song" on *The Fleischmann Hour* 10/27/38, Red Skelton (radio debut) on *The Fleischmann Hour* 8/37. NBC (25 min) #26

1957:

Jan.   "A Tribute to Humphrey Bogart." George Fisher (narrator), John Huston, Joan Davis, excerpts from 1942 *Sealtest Show*, movie *The African Queen.* NBC (30 min.)

1/9   *Recollections at 30* Gene Autry, Tommy Riggs & Betty Lou (radio debut) on *The Fleischmann Hour* 8/5/37, Lillian Roth, Tom Dorsey (radio debut) on *The Magic Key* 11/3/35. NBC (25 min.) #29

2/13   *Recollections at 30* Alexander Woollcott, Raymond Massey "Abe Lincoln in Illinois" on *The Fleischmann Hour*, 1938. NBC (25 min.) #34

2/20   *Recollections* (new title/same show) Jessica Dragonette, Helen Hayes, Vincent Price, The Stroud Twins (radio debut) on *The Fleischmann Hour*, Al Jolson. NBC (25 min.) #35

2/27   *Recollections* Harriet Hilliard, Bob Burns, Elsie Janis, Gene

Raymond, Bob Burns on *The Fleischmann Hour* 7/11/35. NBC (25 min) #36

3/6   *Recollections* Charles Laughton, Babe Didrickson Zaharias, John Boles, Ray Heatherton on *The Fleischmann Hour* 4/37, Harry Lauder, Dinah Shore (radio debut) on *The Eddie Cantor Show* 10/2/40. NBC (25 min.) #37

3/13   *Recollections* Milton Berle on *The Fleischmann Hour* 6/4/36, Eleanor Powell, John Barrymore, Fats Waller on *The Fleischmann Hour*, Mary Martin (radio debut) on *The Royal Gelatin Hour* 2/39. NBC (25 min.) #38

3/20   *Recollections* Beatrice Lillie, Morton Downey, Ignace Paderewski (debut). RV introduces John McCormack 1938. NBC (25 min.) #39

5/8   *Recollections* Gene Austin, Jack Smith, Don McNeill. #46. Last show of the series, NBC (25 min.)

1958:

1/19   Interview (14 min.)

1959:

Date?   *Johnny Presents Philip Morris.* Announcer Johnny's 25th anniversary in radio. Ben Grauer (host), Eddie Cantor, Phil Harris, Horace Heidt, Milton Berle, Marlene Dietrich. NBC (30 min.)

Major Edward Bowes

1962:

Date?   "Twenty Five Years of Progress" of the American

Cancer Society. Bob Considine (host), excerpts from 1937 broadcasts include: Edward Bowes, Fred Allen, W.C. Fields, and Bob Hope. Syndicated (15 min.)

1963:

Nov   *Fidler Now Talks Music* Jimmy Fidler gossips: Tony Martin, The Limelighters, RV's comeback. Syndicated (15 min.)

1964:

11/15   *The Chase and Sanborn Anniversary Show* Edgar Bergen, Maurice Chevalier, Eddie Cantor, Jimmy Durante, W.C. Fields, Rosalind Russell, Mae West, Dorothy Lamour, Nelson Eddy. NBC (60 min.)

1969:

Date?   *That Other Generation* "Feuds and Fights in a Decade of Furors." Documentary about the political and economic feuds during the Great Depression. RV (host), Henry Morgan, Guy Lombardo. WOWO Fort Wayne, Ind., Group W Syndication (30 min.) #1

1986:

7/14   *Same Time, Same Station* "A Tribute to Rudy Vallée." John and Larry Gassman (hosts) KPCC, Los Angeles (1 hr.)

Frank Bresee was host and creator of *The Golden Days of Radio*. Rudy was frequently a guest and listeners were entertained with excerpts from his past radio programs.

Bresee did a two-part tribute to Rudy in 1971, recorded 6/30/71. 6/30/71 *The Golden Days of Radio* "Salute to Rudy Vallée." 2-part tribute to RV and his career. Frank Bresee (host)

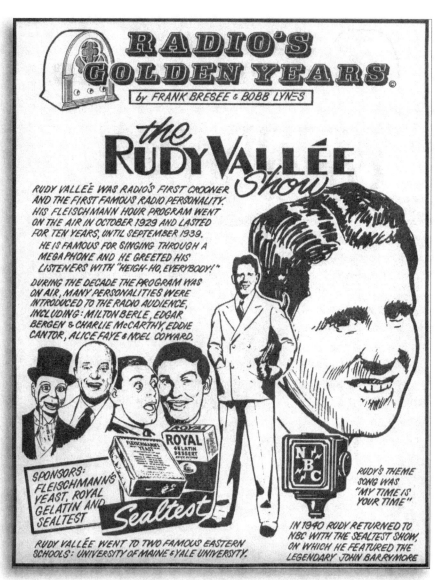

(copyrighted @courtesy: Frank Bresee)

Part 1: Interviews and discussion with RV, excerpts from *The Fleischmann Hour* shows with Joe Penner, Carmen Miranda, Tommy Riggs and Betty Lou, Jack Pearl. Songs: "I'm Just a Vagabond Lover" and "My Time is Your Time." Armed Forces Network (30 min.)

Part 2: Interviews and discussion with RV, excerpts from 1930s and '40s shows with Frank Sinatra, Fred Allen, John and Lionel Barrymore. Also, a 1962 interview and a 1969 monologue. Songs: "The Whiffenpoof Song" and "Goodnight Sweetheart." Armed Forces Network (30 min.)

Bresee did a five-part "78th Birthday Salute" to RV in 1979. Recorded on April 10, 1979, the air dates were:

7/23/79 #801 Part 1
7/24/79 #802 Part 2
7/25/79 #803 Part 3
7/26/79 #804 Part 4
7/27/79 #805 Part 5

Some of RV's appearances on *The Golden Days of Radio*, and recording dates are:

11/5/71	#251
12/12/75	#361
12/21/75	#406
7/16/77	#487
	#642
	#735
	#786
	#806
	#870
4/25/80	#1000 (RV: guest host)

ON YEAH?! FRANK YOU'RE THE BEST!
AFFECTIONALLY Rudy Vallée 7/22/81

(copyrighted photo @ courtesy: Frank Bresee)

1/7/81   #1183 introduces the weekly series of RV talking about
          and featuring his old programs
1/8/81   #1184 first show in the series, which lasted every
          Thursday for two years through
1/20/83   #1714 last show in series

Other notable appearances of RV on Frank Bresee's shows:

10/10/81 *The Golden Days of Radio* "14th Anniversary Christmas
          Program." RV sings: "Meet Me in Monterey" and "Toy-
          land," and he also appears in a comedy routine. From the

(copyrighted photo @ courtesy: Frank Bresee)

Masquers Club in Hollywood, California (2 hr.) #1430

7/31/82   *The Golden Days of Radio* "15th Anniversary Christmas Program." RV sings: "Hooray for Hollywood." From the Variety Arts Club in Los Angeles, California (2 hr.)

12/23/84   *The Golden Days of Radio* "17th Anniversary Christmas Program." #2178

1/14/85   *The Golden Days of Radio*. Songs: "My Time is Your Time" and "I'm Just a Vagabond Lover." Long discussion with RV about memories of his career, broadcasts and personalities he knew. (1 hr.) #2181

The Silver Screen

1. *Campus Sweethearts* (1929) RKO Distributing, 15 min., b&w

   Rudy's first film was released on March 9, 1930, one of 13 all-talking 2-reelers recorded by RCA Photophone and produced at Gramercy Studios in NYC. Contrary to many reports, Ginger Rogers did not appear in this. As Rudy related in his memoirs, Ginger had been rehearsing in the same studio and he asked to meet her. Rather, his leading lady was a former New Jersey beauty contest winner and young wife of the agent William McCaffrey. This film is believed to be lost — in fact, for years Rudy himself searched for a print, but was only able to find a small clip from it in England.

   Dick Currier (supervisor), J. Leo Meehan (director), Alfred Newman (music director), Rudy sings "Under a Campus Moon." CAST: Rudy Vallée, Joe Sawyer, Joey Ray, Leon Leonard.

2. *Rudy Vallée and His Connecticut Yankees* (1929) Vitaphone Corp., 10 minutes, b&w

   CAST: Rudy Vallée and the Connecticut Yankees, Frank Flynn.

3. *Radio Rhythm* (1929) Paramount Famous Lasky, 9 minutes, b&w

   CAST: Rudy Vallée and the Connecticut Yankees. SONGS: "Honey," "Just Another Memory," "You'll Do It Someday."

4. *The Vagabond Lover* (1929) RKO, 69 minutes, b&w

Rudy's first feature movie, portraying a crooning bandleader who impersonates an impresario. Marie Dressler is great fun in her role as a wealthy eccentric.

Marshall Neilan (director), William LeBaron (producer), James A. Creelman (screenwriter), Louis Sarecky (associate producer). CAST: Rudy Vallée (Rudy Bronson), Sally Blane (Jean), Marie Dressler (Mrs. Whitehall), Charles Sellon (Officer Tuttle), with Nella Walker, Malcolm Waite, Alan Roscoe, Eddie Nugent, Rudy Vallée and the Connecticut Yankees. SONGS: "A Little Kiss Each Morning," "Heigh-Ho Every-

RV with Sally Blane

Original title lobby card, 1929. Rudy's comment on the film: "Good God"

body," "If You Were the Only Girl," "I'll Be Reminded of You," "I Love You, Believe Me I Love You" and "Piccolo Pete."

5. *Glorifying the American Girl* (1930) Paramount Famous Lasky Corp., 96 minutes, b&w and color

Slight plot features Mary Eaton as singer who wants to become a Florenz Ziegfeld *Follies* girl. Supposedly a Follies production, many stars are seen as arriving at the "theatre." Rudy sings "I'm Just a Vagabond Lover."

Millard Webb (director/screenwriter), Monte Bell (producer), J.P. McEvoy (screenwriter), George Folsey (cinematographer). Composers include Irving Berlin, Choreographers include Ted Shawn. CAST:

Mary Eaton (Gloria Hughes), Edward Crandall (Buddy), Sarah Edwards (Mrs. Hughes), Dan Healy (Miller). Seen at or arriving at theatre: Florenz Ziegfeld, Ring Lardner, Jr., Adolph Zukor, Noah Beery, Sr., Texas Guinan, Billie Burke, Irving Berlin. Performers: Helen Morgan, Johnny Weissmuller, Rudy Vallée, Eddie Cantor.

6. *The Stein Song* (1931) Paramount Publix Corp., 10 minutes, b&w
    Rudy Vallée heard (but not seen) singing: The Stein Song." Dave Fleischer, Shamus Culhane (directors), Max Fleischer (producer). CAST: Mae Questel (Betty Boop).

7. *Musical Justice* (1931) Paramount Publix Corp., 10 minutes, b&w
    Comedy in which Rudy sings "A Little Kiss Each Morning" and "Don't Take Her Boop a Doop Away." Aubrey Scotto (director), Samuel Lerner (screenwriter). CAST: Rudy Vallée (Judge), Mae Questel (Betty Boop).

8. *Betty Co-Ed* (1931) Paramount Publix Corp., 10 minutes, b&w
    Fun musical. Rudy sings "Betty Co-ed." Dave Fleischer (director), Max Fleischer (producer). CAST: Rudy Vallée (himself), Connecticut Yankees, Mae Questel (Betty Boop).

9. *Kitty from Kansas City* (1931) Paramount Publix Corp., 10 minutes. b&w
    Sing-along song (with the bouncing ball) "Kitty from Kansas City." Dave Fleischer (director). CAST: Rudy Vallée (himself) and the Connecticut Yankees, Mae Questel (Betty Boop).

10. *Knowmore College* (1932) Paramount Publix Corp., 10 minutes b&w
    A charming "professor," Rudy Vallée, teaches a class of dimwitted students lessons by singing little chanties.

Scene from *Musical Doctor*

Aubrey Scotto (director), Samuel Lerner (writer). CAST: Rudy Vallée and the Connecticut Yankees.

11. *Musical Doctor* (1932), Paramount Publix Corp., 10 minutes, b&w
   Rudy sings: "Keep a Little Song Handy" and "Mammy."
   Ray Cozine (director), Samuel Lerner, Sammy Timberg (writers). CAST: Rudy Vallée (Dr. Vallée), Mae Questel.

12. **Rudy Vallée Melodies** (1932), Paramount Publix Corp., 11 minutes, b&w
   Rudy sings with Betty Boop: "Sing a Little Song." Rudy with sing-alongs: "Deep Night," "Stein Song" and "A Little Kiss Each Morning." Rudy sings solo: "Goodnight Sweetheart." Dave Fleischer (director). CAST: Rudy Vallée, Mae Questel (Betty Boop).

on set of *International House*

13. *International House* (1933) Paramount, 72 minutes, b&w

All-star comedy. Various characters meet at a Shanghai hotel to bid on rights to a new invention (television) called Radioscope. Rudy sings "Thank Heaven for You."

Edward Sutherland (director), Albert E. Lewis (producer), Lou Heifetz & Harrison Greene (story), Lou Heifetz, Francis Martin, Walter De Leon and Neil Brant (screenwriters). CAST: Peggy Hopkins Joyce (herself), Stuart Erwin (Tommy Nash), Sara Maritza (Carol Fortescue), George Burns (Dr. Burns), Gracie Allen (Nurse Allen), Rudy Vallée (himself), W.C. Fields (Professor Quail) with Bela Lugosi, Edmond Breese, Rose Marie, Lumsden Hare, Franklin Pangborn, Cab Calloway and his Orchestra and scores of other familiar faces.

14. *George White's Scandals* (1934) 20th Century-Fox, 78 minutes, b&w.

All-star musical. Alice Faye makes her film debut singing her hit "Nasty Man." RV sings "Hold My Hand," "My Dog Loves Your Dog," "Sweet and Simple" and "Every Day is Father's Day." His rendition of "The Man on The Flying Trapeze" fairly steals the show.

Thornton Freeland, George White, Harry Lachman (directors), George White (producer), Harry Lachman, Jack Yellen (screenwriters), Ray Henderson, Irving Caesar (songwriters). CAST: Rudy Vallée (Jimmy Martin), Alice Faye (Mona Vale), George White (himself), Jimmy Durante (Happy Donnelly), Dixie Dunbar (Patsy Day), Gregory

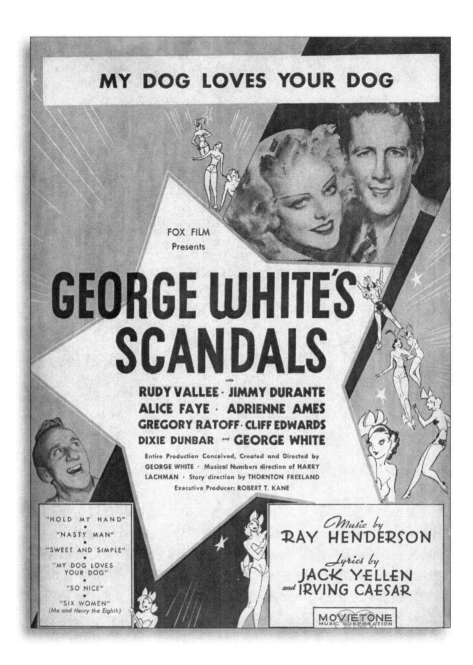

Ratoff (salesman), Adrienne Ames (Barbara Lorraine) with Cliff Edwards, Gertrude Michael, Eleanor Powell, Ned Sparks, James Dunn and dozens more familiar faces in bit parts.

15. *A Trip Through a Hollywood Studio* (1935) 10 minutes, b&w
Moviegoers get a rare inside look at the Warner Bros./First National studio.

Ralph Staub (director), Joe Traub (writer). CAST: William Ray (narrator). With Arthur Aylesworth, Busby Berkeley, James Cagney, Bobby Connolly, Dolores del Rio, Ann Dvorak, Jackie Fields, Hugh Herbert, Jean Muir, Pat O'Brien, Henry O'Neill, Wini Shaw, Rudy Vallée, Alice White, Warren William.

16. *Broadway Highlights No. 1* (1935) Paramount Headliner, 10 minutes, b&w
A short musical comedy mainly featuring stars with stage experience. Fred Waller (director), Milton Hockey (writer). CAST: Max Baer, Jack Benny, Fanny Brice, Earl Carroll, Al Jolson, Beatrice Lillie, Sophie Tucker, Rudy Vallée.

17. *Broadway Highlights No. 2* (1935) Paramount Headliner, 10 minutes, b&w
Another short featuring many opera stars, including an appearance by Italian screen idol Tullio Carminati. Fred Waller (director). CAST: Milton Berle, Tullio Carminati, Floyd Gibbons, Mitzi Green, George Jessel, Benny Leonard, Beatrice Lillie, Grace Moore, Rosa Ponselle, Ed Sullivan, Norma Talmadge, Rudy Vallée, Alice White.

18. *Sweet Music* (1935) Warner Bros., 90 minutes, b&w.
Musical comedy with Rudy appropriately cast as a crooner-bandleader. Exceptional cast includes an appearance by Helen Morgan sing-

ing "I See Two Lovers." Rudy sings "Sweet Music," "There's a Different You," "Ev'ry Day," "Outside," "Good Green Acres," "There's a Tavern in the Town," "Fare Thee Well, Annabelle," also "Selzer Cigar" ad.

Alfred E. Green (director), Sam Bischoff (producer), Jerry Wald, Warren Duff, Carl Erickson (screenwriters). CAST: Rudy Vallée (Skip Houston), Ann Dvorak (Bonnie Haydon), Ned Sparks (Ten Percent Nelson), Helen Morgan (herself), Robert Armstrong (Dopey Malone), Allen Jenkins (Barney Cowan), Alice White (Lulu Betts), Al Shean (Sigmund Selzer), Joseph Cawthorn (Sidney Selzer) with Addison Richards, Philip Reed, Mary Treen, Russell Hicks, Eddie Kane, Milt Kibbee, William B. Davidson, Henry O'Neill, Dave "Tex" O'Brien, Clay Clement, Jack Norton, Milt Britton and his band.

19. *Gold Diggers in Paris* (1938) Warner Bros., 95 minutes, b&w
    (in Britain: *The Gay Imposters*). The last of Warner's *Gold Diggers*
    musicals. In Paris, a New York nightclub company is passed off as a
    ballet troupe. Rudy's songs include "The Latin Quarter," "I Wanna Go
    Back to Bali," "A Stranger in Paree" and "Dreaming All Night Long."
    Ray Enright (director), Sam Bischoff, Hal Wallis (producers), Earl

Scene from *Sweet Music* with Ann Dvorak

Contrary to this ad, Priscilla Lane did not appear

Baldwin, Warren Duff and Jerry Wald (screenwriters), Busby Berkeley (choreography). CAST: Rudy Vallée (Terry Moore), Rosemary Lane (Kay Morrow), Hugh Herbert (Maurice Giraud), Allen Jenkins (Duke Dennis), Gloria Dickson (Mona) with Melville Cooper, Mabel Todd, Edward S. Brophy, Curt Bois, Georges Renevant, Armand Kaliz, Victor Moore, Eddie "Rochester" Anderson, Maurice Cass, Fritz Feld, Victor Kilian, Carole Landis (bit).

20. *For Auld Lang Syne* (1938) Warner Bros., 7 minutes, b&w
This annual Will Rogers Memorial Fund feature was mc-ed by James Cagney, who introduced dozens of Warner Brothers stars.
CAST: (alphabetically) John Barrymore, Freddie Bartholomew, Humphrey Bogart, James Cagney, Donald Crisp, Lily Damita, Bette Davis, Glenda Farrell, Louise Fazenda, Errol Flynn, Benny Goodman and his Orchestra, Lionel Hampton, Hugh Herbert, George Jessel, KCBS-Texas Rangers Band, Gene Krupa, Paul Muni, Harmon Nelson, Dick Powell, Basil Rathbone, Adrian Rollini, Rudy Vallée, Hal B. Wallis, Marie Wilson.

MODERN SCREEN

HERE THEY COME ON A MILLION DOLLAR SPREE
TO WAKE AND MAKE AND TAKE PAREE!

Those gorgeous "Gold Digger" lovelies have taken America twice! Now see what they do to 50 million Frenchmen!

"GOLD DIGGERS IN PARIS"

HEAR ... for the first time on the screen The SCHNICKELFRITZ BAND

& 4 Brilliant Song Hits
"Day Dreaming" · "A Stranger in Paris" · "The Latin Quarter"
"I Wanna Go Back to Bali"

Starring
RUDY VALLEE
ROSEMARY LANE · HUGH HERBERT
ALLEN JENKINS · GLORIA DICKSON
MELVILLE COOPER · MABEL TODD · FRITZ FELD
Directed by RAY ENRIGHT · Screen Play by Earl Baldwin and
Warren Duff · Story by Jerry Wald, Richard Macaulay, Maurice Leo
From an Idea by Jerry Horwin and James Seymour · Music and Lyrics
by Harry Warren and Al Dubin · A WARNER BROS. PICTURE

9

21. *Second Fiddle* (1939), 20th Century-Fox, 85 minutes, b&w

Filmed as a vehicle for Olympic skater Sonja Henie. A studio-initiated romance between Henie and Rudy Vallée fails as it becomes apparent he prefers lovely Mary Healy, while Tyrone Power is pining for Sonja. Rudy sings the Irving Berlin song "I Poured My Heart into a Song," which was nominated for best song of 1939. He also sings "An Old Fashioned Tune" and "When Winter Comes."

Sidney Lanfield (director), Darryl F. Zanuck (producer), Gene Markey (associate producer), Harry Tugend (screenwriter), George Bradshaw (story), Harry Losee (choreography). CAST: Tyrone Power (Jimmy Sutton), Rudy Vallée (Roger Maxwell), Sonja Henie (Trudi Hovland), Mary Healy (Jean Varick), Edna May Oliver (Aunt Phoebe Hovland), Lyle Talbot (Willie Hogger), Alan Dinehart (George "Whit" Whitney), Minna Gombell (Jenny) with Stewart Reburn, Spencer Charters, John Hiestand, George Chandler, Irving Bacon, Maurice Cass, Lillian Porter, Robert Lowery, Frank Coghlan, Jr., The Brian Sisters, The King Sisters.

22. *Rodeo Dough* (1940) Warner Bros., 10 minutes, b&w

A rodeo-centered short. Especially noteworthy for the final appearance of Western superstar Tom Mix, who would die October 12, 1940 in an Arizona car crash.

Sammy Lee (director), Marion Mack (screenplay). CAST: Sally Payne (Sally), Mary Treen (Mary) with Gene Autry, Joe E. Brown, Jackie Cooper, Tom Mix, Tom Neal, Roy Rogers, Mickey Rooney, Rudy Vallée, Johnny Weissmuller.

23. *Take Me Back to My Boots and Saddle* (1941) 3 minutes, b&w

Another short with a Western theme, starring Rudy singing the title song. CAST: Carson Robinson and His Buckaroos (themselves), Rudy Vallée (vocalist), Pearl Pickens (vocalist), Carson Robinson (group leader), Billy Mitchell, John Mitchell (guitarists).

Joan Merrill with RV in *Time Out For Rhythm*

24. *Time Out for Rhythm* (1941) Columbia, 75 minutes, b&w.

A musical comedy with a slight plot involving two theatrical agents planning television specials. Mostly a vehicle for the many specialty numbers, including the Three Stooges' "Maharaja" routine.

Sidney Salkow (director), Irving Starr (producer), Bert Granet (story), Edmund Hartmann, Bert Lawrence (screenwriters), LeRoy Prinz (choreography), based on Alex Ruben's play *Show Business*. CAST: Ann Miller (Kitty Brown), Rudy Vallée (Daniel Collins), Rosemary Lane (Frances Lewis), Allen Jenkins (Off-Beat Davis), Joan Merrill (herself), Richard Lane (Mike Armstrong) with Stanley Andrews, Six Hits and a Miss, The Three Stooges (Larry Fine, Moe Howard and Jerry "Curly" Howard), Eddie Durant's Rhumba Orchestra, Glen Gray and His Casa Loma Orchestra.

on set of *Too Many Blondes*

25. *Picture People No. 2: Hollywood Sports* (1941) RKO, 9 minutes, b&w

Yet another short by a studio to publicize its players; narrated by Helen Broderick, mother of actor Broderick Crawford.

M. Clay Adams (director/writer). CAST: Helen Broderick (narrator), Constance Bennett, Billie Burke, James Craig, Guy Kibbee, Gail Patrick, Nat Pendleton, Roy Rogers, Gilbert Roland, Claire Trevor, Rudy Vallée.

26. *Too Many Blondes* (1941) Universal, 60 minutes, b&w

Romantic comedy centering on a husband and wife radio team with marital problems.

Thornton Freeland (director), Joseph Sanford (producer), Maxwell Shane (story), Louis Kaye, Maxwell Shane (screen-writers). CAST: Rudy Vallée (Dick Kerrigan), Helen Parrish (Virginia Kerrigan), Lon Chaney, Jr., (Marvin Gimble), Jerome Cowan (Ted Bronson), Shemp Howard (hotel manager), Iris Adrian (Hortense), Eddie Quillan (Wally Pelton) with Irving Bacon, Paco Moreno, Dorothy Lee, Gus Schilling.

27. *Happy Go Lucky* (1942) Paramount, 80 minutes, b&w & color

This musical comedy finds Mary Martin in the Caribbean looking to land a rich husband. High point of the film is Betty Hutton belting out "Murder, He Says." Rudy introduces a persona that would follow

throughout the rest of his movie career – the stuffy suitor.

Curtis Bernhardt (director), Harold Wilson (producer), Walter De Leon, Melvin Frank, John Jacolby, Norman Panama (screenwriters), Michael Uris (story), Frank Loesser, Jimmy McHugh, Henry Sayers (songwriters), Paul Oscard (choreography). CAST: Mary Martin (Marjory

Stuart), Dick Powell (Pete Hamilton), Betty Hutton (Bubbles Hennessy), Eddie Bracken (Wally Case), Rudy Vallée (Alfred Monroe) with Mabel Paige, Clem Bevans, Frances Raymond, Irving Bacon, Arthur Loft, Paul McVey, Kay Linaker, Eric Blore, Hillary Brooke.

28. *Hedda Hopper's Hollywood No. 6* (1942) 9 minutes, b&w
Former actress-turned-gossip columnist Hedda Hopper introduces a variety of "friends."

Herbert Moulton (director). CAST: Hedda Hopper (narrator), Joan Bennett, Billy Bletcher, The Canadian Legion Post Band, Claudette Colbert, Joan Davis, Reginald Denny, June Duprez, Hazel Forbes, Reginald Gardiner, Ann Gillis, June Havoc, Ian Hunter, Frieda Inescort, Boris Karloff, Lola Lane, Anita Louise, Joyce Mathews, Adolphe Menjou, Helen Virginia Meyer, Ona Munson, Mary Pickford, Basil Rathbone, Mack Sennett, Mal St. Clair, Rudy Vallée, Ben Webster, Patricia Whitehead, Dame May Whitty.

29. *The Palm Beach Story* (1942), Paramount, 88 minutes, b&w
Screwball comedy with a great cast but Rudy almost steals the movie, receiving an Acting Award from the National Board of Review. However, his vagabond lover image is wounded in the process. Rudy sings "Goodnight Sweetheart" and a bit of "Isn't it Romantic?"

Preston Sturges (director, screenwriter), Paul Jones (producer), Irene (costume design). CAST: Claudette Colbert (Gerry Jeffers), Joel McCrea (Tom Jeffers), Rudy Vallée (John D. Hackensacker III), Mary Astor (Princess Centimellia), William Demarest, Jack Norton, Robert Greig, Roscoe Ates, Dewey Robinson, Chester Conklin (members of Ale and Quail Club), Robert Dudley (Wienie King). A large cast also includes Franklin Pangborn, Robert Warwick, Monte Blue, Esther Howard, and Fred (Snowflake) Toones.

30. *Screen Snapshots Series 23, No. 1: Hollywood in Uniform* (1943) 10 minutes, b&w

Joel McCrea, Mary Astor Claudette Colbert, RV

It's World War II and this is a worthy salute to a few of the men who served in the military.

Ralph Staub (director). CAST: (alphabetically) Eddie Albert, Desi Arnaz, Gene Autry, Art Baker, John Carroll, Jackie Cooper, Glenn Ford, Clark Gable, Van Heflin, John Howard, Alan Ladd, George Montgomery, Wayne Morris, John Payne, Tyrone Power, Gene Raymond, Ronald Reagan, Charles "Buddy" Rogers, Robert Stack, James Stewart, Rudy Vallée.

31. *Rudy Vallée and His Coast Guard Band* (1944) Warner Brothers, 22 minutes.

Produced with the co-operation of the United States Coast Guard, under the direction of Lieutenant Rudy Vallée. Band plays music of different branches of the U.S. military service. Rudy sings "There's Something About a Sailor."

Bobby Connolly (director), Louis Lewyn (producer). CAST: Rudy Vallée and His Coast Guard Band.

32. *It's In the Bag* (1945) United Artists, 90 minutes, b&w

Comedy in which Fred Allen discovers he has inherited millions of dollars but the money has been stuffed in one of the thirteen chairs he has already sold. Rudy sings (along with Don Ameche, Fred Allen and

Victor Moore) "You Made Me What I Am Today."

Richard Wallace (director), Jack H. Skirball (producer), Fred Allen, Jay Dratler and Alma Reville (screenwriters), Morrie Ryskind (story), Based on novel *The Twelve Chairs* by Elie Ilf and Eugene Petrov. CAST: Fred Allen (Fred Floogle), Jack Benny (himself), William Bendix (himself), Binnie Barnes (Eve Floogle), Robert Benchley (Parker), Minerva Pious (Mrs. Nussbaum), Jerry Colonna (Psychiatrist), Rudy Vallée (singer), Don Ameche (guest) with Gloria Pope, William Terry, Sidney Toler, John Carradine, Victor Moore. Radio fans may catch the familiar voice of Walter Tetley as the elevator operator.

33. *Man Alive* (1945) RKO, 70 minutes, b&w

A farcical comedy – Pat O'Brien, convinced that his wife (Ellen Drew) is in love with Rudy Vallée, lets her believe he (O'Brien) is dead.

Ray Enright (director), Robert M. Fellows (producer), Theron Worth (associate producer), Edwin Blum (screenwriter), Jerry Cady and John Tucker Battle (story). CAST: Pat O'Brien (Speed), Adolphe Menjou (Kismet), Ellen Drew (Connie), Rudy Vallée (Gordon Tolliver) with Jonathan Hale, Jack Norton, Minna Gombell, Jason Robards, Sr., Fortunio Bonanova, Gertrude Short, Carl Switzer, Myrna Dell, Joseph Crehan, Robert Clarke, Don Gift, Robert E. Homans.

34. *The Fabulous Suzanne* (1946) Republic, 70 minutes, b&w

Having made money betting on horses, Barbara Britton goes to New York to try her unorthodox methods on the stock market in this romantic comedy. One of the movie's best scenes is Rudy Vallée making fun of a singer (also played by Rudy).

Director/Producer: Steve Sekely (director/producer), Tedwell Chapman and Randall H. Faye (screenwriters/story). CAST: Barbara Britton (Suzanne), Rudy Vallée (Hendrick Courtney, Jr.), Otto Kruger (Hendrick Courtney, Sr.), Richard Denning (Rex), Veda Ann Borg (Mary) with Grady Sutton, Harry Tyler, Eddy Fields, Alvin Hammer, Frank Darien, William Henry.

35. *People Are Funny* (1946) Paramount/Pine Thomas, 94 minutes, b&w

A musical comedy based on the popular radio show in which contestants do silly things for large prizes.

Sam White (director/producer), David Lang, Maxwell Shane (screenwriters), David Lang (story), Jack Crosby (choreography). CAST: Jack Haley (Pinky Wilson), Helen Walker (Corey Sullivan), Rudy Vallée (Ormsby Jamison), Ozzie Nelson (Leroy Brinker), Philip Reed (John Guedel) with Bob Graham, Art Linkletter (as himself), Clara Blandick, Roy Atwell, Wheaton Chambers, Casey Johnson, The Vagabonds, Lillian Molieri, (future Stooge) Joe DeRita, Frances Langford.

36. *The Sin of Harold Diddlebock* (1947) United Artists, 90 minutes, b&w *Mad Wednesday* (1950) RKO/Howard Hughes, re-released in shorter 79-minute version.

Harold Lloyd is a football hero in 1925 and is offered a job in a bank. Twenty-two years later he is a weary clerk who is abruptly fired one Wednesday morning. What happens on that "mad Wednesday" makes for a typically funny Lloyd movie. When released in 1947 it did well but co-producer (Hughes) was not pleased and withdrew the film. He spent nearly four years rewriting and cutting until releasing it again in the shortened version in 1950. The latter version works well but the original should not be missed for its pure Sturges touch.

Preston Sturges (director/producer/screenwriter: 1947); Howard Hughes (co-producer). CAST: Harold Lloyd (Harold Diddlebock), Al Bridge (Wild Bill Hitchcock), Frances Ramsden (Miss Otis), Raymond Walburn (E.J. Waggleberry), Georgia Caine (bearded lady), Jimmy Conlin (Wormy), Franklin Pangborn (Formfit Franklin), Margaret Hamil-

ton (Flora), Edgar Kennedy (Jake) with (in the huge cast) Arthur Hoyt, Arline Judge, Torben Meyer, Frank Moran, Jack Norton, Lionel Stander, Rudy Vallée as a banker.

37. *The Bachelor and the Bobby-Soxer* (1947), RKO, 95 minutes, b&w

Romantic comedy in which Judge Myrna Loy sentences Cary Grant to romance her sister, Shirley Temple, hoping to cure the latter of her crush. Eventually she realizes she wants Grant instead of her stuffy district attorney beau played (in what is now his usual character) by Rudy Vallée. Won 1947 Academy Award for best original screenplay.

Irving G. Reis (director), Dore Schary (producer), Sidney Sheldon (screenwriter). CAST: Myrna Loy (Judge Margaret Turner), Cary Grant (Dick Nugent), Shirley Temple (Susan Turner), Irving Bacon (Melvin), William Bakewell (Winters), Rudy Vallée (Tom Chamberlain), Ian Bernard (Perry), Veda Ann Borg (Agnes Prescott), Ray Collins (Matt Beemish) with Harry Davenport, Gregory Gaye, William Hall, Carol Hughes, Lillian Randolph, Johnny Sands, Ransom Sherman, William Forest, Dan Tobin, Don Beddoe.

38. *Unfaithfully Yours* (1947), 20th Century-Fox, 105 minutes, b&w

Dark romantic comedy starring Rex Harrison as a conductor who becomes convinced his wife (Linda Darnell) is unfaithful. During concerts he imagines all the

RV, Barbara Lawrence, Kurt Kreuger, Lionel Stander

ways he will punish her, including murder. Rudy's role is even less sympathetic than usual.

Preston Sturges (director/producer/screenwriter). CAST: Rex Harrison (Alfred De Carter), Linda Darnell (Daphne De Carter), Barbara Lawrence (Barbara Henshler), Rudy Vallée (August Henshler), Kurt Kreuger (Anthony), Lionel Stander (Hugo Standoff), Edgar Kennedy (Detective Sweeney) with Alan Bridge, Julius Tannen, Torben Meyer, Robert Greig, Evelyn Beresford, Georgia Caine, Harry Seymour, Isabel Jewell, Marion Marshall, Frank Moran.

39. *I Remember Mama* (1948), RKO, 95 minutes, b&w
Drama about an immigrant family in early 20th-century San Francisco

struggling with poverty and family difficulties. Vallée's role, though not large, was noted and praised by critics.   Dunne, Bel Geddes, Homolka and Corby all were nominated for Oscars. Corby won 1949 Golden Globe as Best Supporting Actress.

George Stevens (director), George Stevens, Harriet Parsons (producers), DeWitt Bodeen (screenwriter), based on John Van Druten's play which he adapted from Kathryn Forbes' book, *Mama's Bank Account*. CAST: Irene Dunne (Mama Hansen), Barbara Bel Geddes (Katrin Hansen), Philip Dorn (Papa Hansen), Oscar Homolka (Uncle Chris), Cedric Hardwicke (Mr. Hyde), Rudy Vallée (Dr. Johnson), Edgar Bergen (Peter Thorkelson), Ellen Corby (Aunt Trina), Hope Landin (Aunt Jenny), Edith Evanson (Aunt Sigrid), Barbara O'Neil (Jessie Brown), Peggy McIntyre (Christina Hansen), June Hedin (Dagmar Hansen), Steve Brown (Nels Hansen), Tommy Ivo (Cousin Arne) with Cleo Ridgely, Constance Purdy, Franklin Farnum, Ruth Tobey, Stanley Andrews, Lela Bliss, Florence Bates.

40. *So This is New York* (1948) United Artists, 80 minutes, b&w Re-released in 1953 as *Broadway Guys*

This comedy finds Henry Morgan inheriting a small fortune and taking his family to New York City. Various oddball characters they meet would all like a piece of the inheritance and start courting Morgan's pretty sister-in-law Dona Drake. Rudy gets to play a role that is fun and romantic for a change!

Richard Fleischer (director), Stanley Kramer (producer), Herbert Baker, Carl Foreman (screenwriters), based on "The Big Town," a collection of stories by Ring Lardner. CAST: Henry Morgan (Ernie Finch), Virginia Grey (Ella Finch), Dona Drake (Kate Goff), Rudy Vallée (Herbert Daley), Bill Goodwin (Jimmy Ralston), Leo Gorcey (Sid Mercer), Jerome Cowan (Francis Griffin) with David Willock, Frank Orth, Arnold Stang, Hugh Herbert, William Bakewell.

Dona Drake and RV

41. *My Dear Secretary* (1948) United Artists, 94 minutes, color

Yet another romantic comedy – aspiring writer Laraine Day becomes the secretary to womanizer Kirk Douglas. Rudy Vallée is (again!) a stuffy suitor. Keenan Wynn nearly steals the movie with his sardonic wit.

Charles Martin (director/screenwriter), Leo C. Popkin (producer), Harry M. Popkin (executive producer). CAST: Laraine Day (Stephanie Gaylord), Kirk Douglas (Owen Waterbury), Helen Walker (Elsie), Keenan Wynn (Ronnie Hastings), Rudy Vallée (Charles Harris), Florence Bates (Mrs. Reeves), Alan Mowbray (Deveny), Grady Sutton (Scott), Irene Ryan (Mary), Gale Robbins (Dawn O'Malley) with Virginia Hewitt, Abe Reynolds, Jody Gilbert, Helene Stanley, Joe Kirk, Russell Hicks, Gertrude Astor, Martin Lamont, Charles Halton.

42. *Mother is a Freshman* (1949) 20th Century-Fox, 81 minutes, color
British title: *Mother Knows Best*

Widowed Loretta Young is going back to college along with her coed daughter, Betty Lynn. Complications arise when they both set their sights on the same professor (Van Johnson). Alas, Rudy is again that stuffy suitor in another romantic comedy.

Lloyd Bacon (director), Walter Morosco (producer), Mary Loos, Richard Sale (screenwriters), Raphael Blau (story). CAST: Loretta Young (Abigail Abbott), Van Johnson (Richard Michaels), Rudy Vallée (Prof. John Heaslip), Betty Lynn (Susan Abbott), Barbara Lawrence (Louise Sharp), Robert Arthur (Beaumont Jackson) with Griff Barnett, Kathleen Hughes, Eddie Dunn, Claire Meade, Virginia Brissac, Charles Lane, Kathryn Card, Marietta Canty, Debra Paget, Robert Patten.

43. *The Beautiful Blonde from Bashful Bend* (1949) 20th Century-Fox, 77 minutes, color

Enjoyable Western-comedy in which dance-hall girl Betty Grable arrives at Bashful Bend and is mistaken for the expected schoolmarm. She immediately sets her sights on the wealthy banker, who else but Rudy Vallée! A colorful cast of supporting players (a Sturges trademark) fairly steals the film. Sturges' final American film is appreciated more now than it was fifty years ago.

Preston Sturges (director/producer/screenwriter), Earl Felton (story). CAST: Betty Grable (Freddie Jones/Hilda Swandumper), Cesar Romero (Blackie Jobero), Rudy Vallée (Charles Hingleman), Olga San Juan (Conchita), Sterling Holloway & Danny Jackson (Basserman Boys), Hugh Herbert (doctor), El Brendel (Mr. Jorgensen), Porter Hall (Judge O'Toole), Pati Behrs (Roulette), Margaret Hamilton (Elvira O'Toole) with Emory Parnell, Al Bridge, Chris-Pin Martin, John Farrell McDonald, Richard Hale, Georgia Caine, Esther Howard, Harry Hayden, Chester Conklin, Torben Meyer, Dewey Robinson, Richard Kean, Harry Ty-

Olga San Juan, RV, Betty Grable, Sterling Holloway

ler, Dudley Dickerson, Russell Simpson, Marie Windsor, Mary Monica McDonald.

44. *Father Was a Fullback* (1949) 20th Century-Fox, 84 minutes, b&w
    Football coach Fred MacMurray's team can't win a game, putting his job at risk. All works out when a football champ arrives, thanks to daughter Betty Lynn. Rudy Vallée replays his usual stuffy role in this light comedy.
    John M. Stahl (director), Fred Kohlmar (producer), Aleen Leslie, Mary Loos, Casey Robinson, Richard Sale (screenwriters), from the play by Clifford Goldsmith. CAST: Fred MacMurray (George Cooper),

Maureen O'Hara (Elizabeth Cooper), Betty Lynn (Connie Cooper), Rudy Vallée (Mr. Jessup), Thelma Ritter (Geraldine), Natalie Wood (Ellen Cooper), Richard Tylar (Joe Birch) with Forbes Murray, Buddy Martin, Mickey McCardle, Bill Self, Charles Flynn, Joe Haworth, Jim Backus, Robert Patten.

45. *The Admiral Was a Lady* (1950), United Artists, 87 minutes, b&w
In this romantic comedy Wanda Hendrix is a WAVE officer trying to save her boyfriend from fiendish millionaire Rudy Vallée. All the time she is being pursued by ex-airman Edmond O'Brien. An enjoyable film with an unbelievable plot.

Albert Rogell (director), Jack Warner (producer), John O'Dea, Sidney Salkow (screenwriters). CAST: Wanda Hendrix (Jean Madison), Edmond O'Brien (Jim Stevens), Rudy Vallée (Mr. Pettigrew), Johnny

with Marjorie Main in *Ricochet Romance*

Sands (Eddie), Steve Brodie (Mike), Richard Erdman (Ollie), Hillary Brooke (Mrs. Pettigrew), Richard Lane (fight promoter), Gary Owen (detective), Fred Essler (shopkeeper).

46. *Ricochet Romance* (1954) Universal, 80 minutes, b&w

This comedy finds new cook Marjorie Main planning to restore a rundown dude ranch, putting everyone to work toward that end. This includes a shiftless handyman played by Chill Wills, for whom she also has romantic plans.

Charles Lamont (director), Robert Arthur, Richard Wilson (producers), Kay Lenard (screenwriter). CAST: Marjorie Main (Pansy Jones), Chill Wills (Tom Williams), Pedro Gonzalez-Gonzalez (Manuel Gonzales), Alfonso Bedoya (Alfredo Gonzales), Ruth Hampton (Angela Ann Mansfield), Benay Venuta (Claire Renard), Judith Ames (Betsy Williams), Darryl Hickman (Dave King), Lee Aaker (Timmy Williams), Irene Ryan (Miss Clay), Rudy Vallée (Worthington Higgenmacher) with Philip Tonge, Phil Chambers, Charles Watts, Marjorie Bennett.

47. *Gentlemen Marry Brunettes* (1955) United Artists, 95 minutes, color

Two Broadway chorus girls travel to Paris in search of love and adventure in this romantic musical. Their mother and aunt had done the same thing in the 1920s, at which time they had both been romanced by Rudy Vallée. Songs by Rudy: "Have You Met Miss Jones?" and "I Wanna Be Loved by You."

Richard Sale (director/producer/screenwriter), Robert Waterfield (co-producer), Robert Bassler (executive producer), Mary Loos (screenwriter), Jack Cole (choreography), from book *But Gentlemen Marry Brunettes* by Anita Loos. CAST: Jeanne Crain (Connie/Mitzi Jones), Jane Russell (Bonnie/Mimi Jones), Alan Young (Charlie Biddle/Mr./Mrs. Biddle), Scott Brady (David Action), Rudy Vallée (himself), Guy Middleton (Earl of Wickenware), Eric Pohlmann (Monsieur Ballard), Leonard Sachs (Monsieur Duty), Guido Lorraine (Monsieur Marcel) with Derek Sydney, Robert Favart, Duncan Elliot, Maurice Lane, Michael Balfour, Ferdinand Mayne, Boyd Caheen.

48. *Jazz Ball* (1956) Republic Pictures, 60 minutes, b&w

An unusual Republic documentary featuring a variety of music greats. Performers include Red Nichols, The Mills Brothers, Peggy Lee, Buddy Rich, Artie Shaw and His Band, Rudy Vallée, Cab Calloway, Gene Krupa, Louis Armstrong, Duke Ellington, Betty Hutton.

49. *The Helen Morgan Story* (1957) Warner Bros., 118 minutes, b&w

This drama is supposedly a biography of the life of legendary singer

Jeanne Crain, Scott Brady, Alan Young, Jane Russell, RV

Helen Morgan. Story rewrites her life to give a happy ending, unfortunately not true. Gogi Grant's voice was dubbed-in, despite the fact that star Ann Blyth had a great voice.

Michael Curtiz (director), Martin Rackin (producer), Nelson Gidding, Stephen Longstreet, Dean Riesner, Oscar Sau (screenwriters). CAST: Ann Blyth (Helen Morgan), Paul Newman (Larry), Richard Carlson (Wade), Gene Evans (Whitney Krause), Alan King (Ben) with Cara Williams, Virginia Vincent, Walter Wolf King, Dorothy Green, Warren Douglas, Sammy White, Edward Platt, Iris Adrian. Playing themselves: Jimmy McHugh, Rudy Vallée, Walter Winchell.

50. *How to Succeed in Business Without Really Trying* (1967) United

Artists, 121 minutes, color

Window-washer Robert Morse reads a book about how to climb the corporate ladder without work in this musical comedy. Rudy Vallée recreated his Broadway role as company president J. B. Biggley.

David Swift (director/producer/screenwriter), from play *How to Succeed in Business Without Really Trying* by Abe Burrows, Willie Gilbert, Jack Weinstock, play adapted from book of same name by Shepherd Mead. CAST: Robert Morse (J. Pierpont Finch), Michele Lee (Rosemary Pilkington), Rudy Vallée (J. B. Biggley), Anthony Teague (Bud Frump), Maureen Arthur (Hedy LaRue), Murray Matheson (Benjamin Ovington), Sammy Smith (Wally Womper) also in the huge cast Kay Reynolds, John Myers, Jeff deBenning, Ruth Kobart, Robert Q. Lewis, George Fenneman, Anne Seymour, Joey Faye, Hy Averback, Erin O'Brien-Moore.

51. *Silent Treatment* (1968) color (Unfinished)

This proposed all-star film was never completed, and actress Phyllis Diller has no memory of the project.

Ralph Andrews (director). CAST (proposed): Gene Autry, Milton Berle, Jackie Coogan, Phyllis Diller, John Forsythe, Marty Ingels, Sherry Jackson, Jerry Lewis, Paul Lynde, George Raft, Aldo Ray, Forrest Tucker, Rudy Vallée.

52. *Live a Little, Love a Little* (1968) MGM, 90 minutes, color

A slight storyline in this romantic musical, the only interest being the appearance of the love idol of the 1930s, Rudy Vallée, opposite the ditto (Elvis Presley) of the 1960s. Rather unmemorable songs include "Wonderful World," "Edge of Reality," "A Little Less Conversation" and "Almost in Love."

Norman Taurog (director), Douglas Laurence (producer), Dan Greenburg, Michael A. Hoey (screenwriters), from book *Kiss My Firm But Pliant Lips* by Dan Greenburg. CAST: Elvis Presley (Greg), Michele Carey (Bernice), Rudy Vallée (Penlow), Don Porter (Lansdown),

femme idols 1938 and 1968

Dick Sargent (Harry), Sterling Holloway (milkman), Celeste Yarnell (Ellen), Eddie Hodges (delivery boy) with Joan Shawlee, Emily Banks, Edie Baskin, John Hegner, Ursula Menzel, Merri Ashley.

53. *The Night They Raided Minsky's* (1968) United Artists, 97 minutes, color

A Quaker girl comes to New York to get a job dancing in Biblical interpretations. Ending up at Minsky's burlesque house, she accidentally invents the striptease while doing Salome's dance of the seven veils! There are subplots galore in this delightful comedy.

William Friedkin (director), Bud Yorkin, Norman Lear (producer), Norman Lear, Sidney Michaels, Arnold Schulman (screenwriters), book by Rowland Barber, *The Night They Raided Minsky's*. Rudy Vallée (Narrator). CAST: Jason Robards, Jr. (Raymond Paine), Britt Ekland (Rachel Schpitendavel), Norman Wisdom (Chick Williams), Forrest Tucker (Trim Houlihan), Harry Andrews (Jacob Schpitendavel), Joseph Wiseman (Louis Minsky), Denholm Elliott (Vance Fowler), Elliott Gould (Billy Minsky), Bert Lahr (Prof. Spats). Also in the huge cast: Jack Burns, Gloria LeRoy, Lillian Hayman, Herbie Faye, Judith Lowry.

54. *The Phynx* (1970) Warner Bros., 92 minutes, color

A meant-to-be-campy cold war comedy, with a huge cast of old-time stars. Rudy Vallée plays himself. The film opened in a few theatres and then was withdrawn from release.

Lee Katzin (director), Bob Booker, George Foster (producers), Stan Cornyn (screenwriter), Bob Booker, George Foster (story). CAST: Lonny Stevens (The Phynx), Lou Antonio (Corrigan), Mike Kellin (Bogey), Michael Ansara (Colonel Rostinov), Joan Blondell (Ruby), George Tobias (Markevitch) with Larry Hankin, Ted Eccles, Pat McCormick, Barbara Noonan, and Edgar Bergen, Busby Berkeley, Xavier Cugat, Fritz Feld, George Jessel, Ruby Keeler, Patsy Kelly, Dorothy Lamour, Joe Louis, Maureen O'Sullivan, Jay Silverheels, Ed Sullivan, Rudy Vallée.

55. *Slashed Dreams* (a.k.a. *Sunburst*) (1974) 74 minutes, color

Violent drama about two girls being stalked and attacked by two deranged woodsmen. Robert Englund would go on to bigger and better (?) things as Freddy Krueger in the *Nightmare on Elm Street* series.

CAST: James Keach, Peter Hooten, Anne Lockhart, David Pritchard, Rudy Vallée, Kathy Baumann, Robert Englund, Peter Brown.

56. *Won Ton Ton, the Dog Who Saved Hollywood* (1976) Paramount, 92 minutes, color

It would seem as if every old-time Hollywood star was called to appear in this comedy. It is a spoof of the great Rin-Tin-Tin and the canine legend!

Michael Winner (director), David Picker (producer). CAST: Bruce Dern (Grayson Potchuk), Madeline Kahn (Estie), Art Carney (J.J. Fromberg), Phil Silvers (Murray), Ron Leibman (Rudy), Teri Garr (Fluffy) and fifty+ old-time stars including Joan Blondell, John Carradine, Dennis Day, Yvonne de Carlo, Andy Devine, Alice Faye, Rhonda Fleming, Tab Hunter, Dorothy Lamour, Jack LaRue, Keye Luke, Victor Mature, Virginia Mayo, Ethel Merman, Ann Miller, Walter Pidgeon, Ritz Brothers, Rudy Vallée.

57. *City Heat* (1984) Warner Bros., 98 minutes, color

Set in 1933, this action drama stars Burt Reynolds and Clint Eastwood in what is almost a parody of their screen personas. Early on, Burt returns to his apartment and flips on the radio as the phone rings. If you listen closely above the dialogue you can hear Rudy Vallée singing "Let's Do It."

Richard Benjamin (director), Fritz Manes (producer), Sam O. Brown, Joseph Stinson (screenwriters), Sam O. Brown (story). CAST: Clint Eastwood (Lt. Speer), Burt Reynolds (Mike Murphy), Madeline Kahn (Caroline) with Jane Alexander, Rip Torn, Irene Cara, Richard Roundtree, William Sanderson.

58. *Miller's Crossing* (1990), 20th Century-Fox, 120 minutes, color

A violent gangland crime-drama set in the Prohibition days of the 1930s. As background to add to the '30s atmosphere we can hear the music of Rudy Vallée, Sonny Burke and Ray Noble.

Joel Coen (director), Ethan Coen, Graham Place, Ben Barenholtz (producers), Ethan Coen, Joel Coen (screenwriters). CAST: Gabriel Byrne (Tom Reagan), Albert Finney (Leo), Marcia Gay Harden (Verna), Jon Polito (Johnny), John Turturro (Bernie).

Into Your Living Room

1. *Toast of the Town,* January 2, 1949, CBS Season 2 / Episode 29

    Ed Sullivan (host), Pat C. Flick (comedian). Guest Stars: Irving Harmon (phone booth routine), The Ravens ("My Sugar is So Refined"), Rudy Vallée, Betty Jane Smith (tap dancer), Bobby Whaling & Yvette (comedic bicycle act). Audience bows: George M. Cohan, Jr., Johnny Farrell, Jersey Joe Wolcott.

    Rudy Vallée makes his television debut with a 10-minute interview by host Sullivan. Rudy leads the audience in a sing-along of "Alouetta" and performs a medley of songs including "I'm Just a Vagabond Lover" and "If You Were the Only Girl in the World."

2. *Toast of the Town,* January 16, 1949, CBS Season 2 / Episode 31

    Ed Sullivan (host). Guest Stars: Rudy Vallée, Nanette Fabray.

3. *Toast of the Town,* February 6, 1949, CBS Season 2 / Episode 34

    Ed Sullivan (host), Jackie Gleason (himself, performs dramatic movie scene). Guest Stars: Luise Rainer (talks about career, does scene from 1935 film *Escapade*), Harry Armstrong (singer, "Sweet Adeline"), W.C. Handy ("St. Louis Blues"), Pat Henning (comedic imitations), William J. McKenna (songwriter, "Has Anybody Here Seen Kelly?"), Marybeth Olds (dancer-contortionist, acrobatic act), Viola Essen & Johnny Coy (tap vs. ballet dance contest), Rudy Vallée (cameo, appears backstage).

4. *Toast of the Town,* February 13, 1949, CBS Season 2 / Episode 35
   Ed Sullivan (host). Guest Stars: Rudy Vallée, Diana Barrymore.

5. *We, the People,* February 15, 1949 Season 2 / Episode 38
   Preston Wood (director), Dwight Weist (host). Guest Stars:
   Eric Johnston, Rudy Vallée, C. Hamilton Moses.

6. *Texaco Star Theater,* February 28, 1950 Season 2 / Episode 79
   Milton Berle (host), Sid Stone (pitchman), Alan Roth (bandleader),
   Fatso Marco. Guest Stars: Victor Jory, Rudy Vallée.

7. *Your Show of Shows,* April 15, 1950, NBC Season 1 / Episode 8
   Regular cast: Sid Caesar, Imogene Coca, Carl Reiner, Jack Russell,
   James Starbuck, The Bob Hamilton Trio, Dick DeFreitas, Bill
   Hayes, Earl Redding, Jerry Ross, Angela Castle, Robert Merrill,
   Billy Williams Quartet. Guest Star: Rudy Vallée.

8. *Toast of the Town,* September 24, 1950, CBS Season 4 / Episode
   119 Ed Sullivan (host). Guest Stars: Gloria Swanson, Rudy Vallée,
   Anna Maria Alberghetti.

9. *What's My Line?,* November 12, 1950, CBS Season 2 / Episode 24
   John Daly (moderator), Lee Vines (announcer), Regular panelists:
   Arlene Francis, Hal Block, Dorothy Kilgallen with Jerry Franken
   (guest panelist), and Rudy Vallée (mystery guest).
   Kinescopes of early television shows were routinely destroyed by CBS
   until 1952 when Gil Fates noticed this policy and began saving them.
   Vallée's first *What's My Line?* appearance, unfortunately, is not one of the
   ten pre-1952 episodes which still survive.

10. *Texaco Star Theater,* November 14, 1950 Season 3 / Episode 103

Milton Berle (host), Sid Stone (pitchman), Alan Roth (bandleader), Fatso Marco. Guest Stars: Chester Morris, Martha Raye, Rudy Vallée, Hal LeRoy, Sandra Berle (Milton's wife).

11. ***Texaco Star Theater,*** December 25, 1951 Season 4 / Episode 148
Milton Berle (host), Alan Roth (bandleader), Fatso Marco. Guest Stars: Risé Stevens, Rudy Vallée.

12. ***Toast of the Town,*** January 13, 1952, CBS Season 5 / Episode 187
"The George White Story, Part 1." Ed Sullivan (host), Art Hannes (announcer). Special Guest: George White, Broadway producer, director, playwright and showman. Guest Stars: Harry Richman (appeared in four George White Broadway productions, 1929-32), Helen Wood, Horace McMahon, Hal LeRoy (dancer), Smith and Dale (comedy team), Richard Hayes (actor), Betty Bruce (singer), Peggy Lee, Rudy Vallée. Songs: "Thank Your Mother," "This is the Mrs.," "My Song," "Are You Having Any Fun?"
Ed Sullivan's *Toast of the Town* presented this special 2-part tribute to Broadway showman George White, with the second part airing on February 17. Vallée participates in the grand finale song "Life is Just a Bowl of Cherries" with Peggy Lee and others.
Guests in part 2 included: Toni Arden (singer), The Costello Twins, Richard Hayes, Danny Hoctor, Harry Richman, Hal LeRoy, Smith and Dale, Frances Williams, Helen Wood. Vallée did not appear.

13. ***Texaco Star Theatre,*** October 21, 1952 Season 5 / Episode 178
Milton Berle (host), Jimmy Nelson (pitchman), Alan Roth (bandleader), Ruth Gilbert, Bobby Sherwood (regulars), Greg Garrison (director). Guest Stars: Rudy Vallée, Mel Tormé, Rose Marie, Roland Young.

George White

14. *The Ford Fiftieth Anniversary Show,* June 15, 1953, CBS/NBC
live performance, 9-11 pm Jerome Robbins (director), Howard
Teichmann (writer), Edward R. Murrow and Oscar Hammerstein
II (hosts), Leland Hayward (producer, introduction), Henry Ford
II (concludes the program with a hope/plea for future world peace
and prosperity). Stars (alphabetically): Marian Anderson, Wally
Cox, Bing Crosby, Eddie Fisher, Miriam Hopkins, Kukla and Ollie
(Burr Tilstrom's puppets), Mary Martin, Ethel Merman, Frank
Sinatra, Lowell Thomas, Rudy Vallée.

The Ford Motor Company celebrated its 50th anniversary by presenting this 2-hour retrospective of the history of the United States and the world in the last half century. Often referred to as the first television spectacular, Ford bought airtime on both CBS and NBC and presented it without commercial interruption.

15. *Toast of the Town,* January 30, 1955, CBS Season 8 / Episode 318 "A Cavalcade of Radio 1920-1955" (based on the book by Ben Gross, *I Looked and I Listened*). Ed Sullivan (host), Art Hannes (announcer). Guest Stars (from NY): Eve Arden, Edward Arnold, Gene Autry, Red Barber, André Baruch, Jack Benny, Gertrude Berg, Edgar Bergen & Charlie McCarthy, Norman Brokenshire, Eddie Cantor, William Conrad, Milton Cross, Jessica Dragonette, The Fitzgeralds, John Gambling, Jay Joslyn, Vincent Lopez, Ted Mack, Edward R. Murrow, Frank Parker, The Pickens Sisters, Peter Potter, Roger Pryor, Robert Rockwell, David Ross, Lanny Ross, George Seaton, George Shelton, Rudy Vallée, Paul Whiteman, Ed Wynn. (from California): Harry Von Zell (host), Jack Bailey, Bob Burns, Ed Gardner, George Givot, Jean Hersholt, Art Linkletter, Ken Murray, J. Carroll Naish, Hal Peary, Ginny Simms, Jimmy Wallington.
   Great shows and historic moments on radio are recreated by stars of stage, screen, radio and music from both Hollywood and New York.

16. *Star Tonight,* June 2, 1955, ABC Season 1 / Episode 18 episode: "Taste." Roald Dahl (writer).Guest Stars: Leonard Elliott, Violet Heming, Diana Millay, Rudy Vallée.

17. *Eddie Cantor Comedy Theatre,* July 25, 1955, ABC Season 1 / Episode 27 episode: "The Playboy." Eddie Cantor (host/star) Guest Star: Rudy Vallée.
   To win the favor of his girlfriend's father, a rich playboy must show he

can hold down a job for one week. This series lasted less than a year, from January 1 to November 1, 1955.

18. *Colgate Comedy Hour,* October 23, 1955 Season 6 / Episode 214
    Jack Carson (host), Robert Finkel (director). Guest Stars: Henry "Red" Sanders (UCLA head coach), Ronnie Knox (UCLA football player), The Bob Hamilton Trio, Jack Haley, Helen Grayco (singer), Mickey Rooney, Stan Freberg, Rudy Vallée, Ray Milland, The Compton College Cornets, and the UCLA Cheerleading Squad.
    As you might deduce from the guest stars, this program is devoted to a salute to football.   Additionally, future Hall-of-Fame sportscaster Mel Allen visits the Los Angeles Rams dressing room and interviews many players.

19. *Shower of Stars,* December 15, 1955 Season 2 / Episode 3 episode: "Gold Records." Jack Benny, William Lundigan (regular cast). Guest Stars: Red Skelton, Rudy Vallée, Frankie Laine, Gene Austin, Eddie "Rochester" Anderson, Gary Crosby.

20. *December Bride,* January 23, 1956, CBS Season 2 / Episode 50 episode: "The Rudy Vallee Show." Verna Felton (Hilda Crocker), Dean Miller (Matt Henshaw), Frances Rafferty (Ruth Henshaw), Harry Morgan (Pete Porter). Guest Star: Rudy Vallée.

21. *The Vic Damone Show,* 1956, CBS Vic Damone (host/star)
    This 30-minute variety show had a brief (13-episode) run as a summer replacement for *December Bride* from July-September 1956 and again in 1957. Rudy Vallée was one of many guest stars including Gene Krupa, Gogi Grant and Arnold Stang.

22. *Matinee Theatre,* December 7, 1956, NBC Season 2 / Episode 275 episode: "Jenny Kissed Me."

23. *Texaco Command Appearance,* 1957, NBC

A short-lived successor to the extremely successful *Texaco Star Theater,* this one-hour variety show was a salute to big-time performers. Comedian Ed Wynn had the honor of being spotlighted on the premiere episode, while Rudy Vallée was featured later in the season.

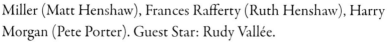

24. *December Bride,* October 7, 1957, CBS Season 4 / Episode 96 episode: "Vallée's Protegé" (a.k.a. "Crashing Hollywood"). Verna Felton (Hilda Crocker), Dean Miller (Matt Henshaw), Frances Rafferty (Ruth Henshaw), Harry Morgan (Pete Porter). Guest Star: Rudy Vallée.

25. *The Lucy-Desi Comedy Hour,* November 6, 1957, CBS Season 1 / Episode 1 episode: "Lucy Takes a Cruise to Havana." Lucille Ball (Lucy Ricardo), Desi Arnaz (Ricky Ricardo), Vivian Vance (Ethel Mertz), William Frawley (Fred Mertz), Keith Thibodeaux (little Ricky Ricardo). Guest Stars: Ann Sothern (Susie MacNamara), Cesar Romero (Carlos Garcia), Rudy Vallée (himself), Hedda Hopper (herself), Frank Nelson (cruise director), George Trevino (judge), Nestor Palva (jailor), Joaquin delRio (trustee), Vincent Padula (nightclub owner)

Lucy and her friend Susie (Ann Sothern) take a cruise to Cuba. On the ship they meet Fred and Ethel (on their honeymoon!) Also on the cruise is Rudy Vallée, who just wants to be left alone – but, of course,

Lucy and Susie won't allow that. In Havana, Lucy meets Desi who wants a singing job in America, which Rudy arranges.

This premiere episode was originally filmed at 75 minutes and co-producer Arnaz was adamant against trimming this length. He convinced the producers of *The U.S. Steel Hour* to relinquish the first 15 minutes of their show, promising it enormous ratings because of the Lucy-Desi lead-in. The original version still exists but reruns invariably feature a 60-minute version, cutting Hedda Hopper's introduction and parts throughout.

26. *I've Got a Secret,* December 4, 1957, CBS Episode 291
   Regular panelists: Bill Cullen, Faye Emerson, Harry Morgan, Jayne Meadows, with Rudy Vallée (guest).

27. *Kraft Television Theatre,* January 1, 1958, NBC   Season 11 / Episode 548 episode: "The Battle for Wednesday Night." William Graham (director), Robert Van Scoyk (writer). Guest Stars: Rudy Vallée, Earl Holliman, Jack Oakie, Virginia Gibson.

28. (Special) *Hansel and Gretel,* April 27, 1958, NBC musical. Music by Alec Wilder, Lyrics by William Engvick. Red Buttons (Hansel), Barbara Cook (Gretel), Risé Stevens (mother), Rudy Vallée (father), Stubby Kaye (town crier), Hans Conried (witch), Paula Laurence (Meenie).

29. *The Jack Paar Show,* 1958, CBS
   Originating in September 1954, *The Tonight Show* was hosted by Steve Allen until January 1957. Jack Paar's reign lasted from July 1957-March 1962, being called *The Jack Paar Show* from 1959 on. In 1959 it became one of the first, if not the very first, regular program in color. Paar's conversationalist

style attracted celebrities from all walks of life; Rudy Vallée made his appearance during the 1958 season on this, his favorite late-night show.

30. ***What's My Line?,*** August 24, 1958, CBS Season 9 / Episode 430
    John Daly (moderator). Regular panelists: Arlene Francis, Bennett Cerf, Dorothy Kilgallen, with Rudy Vallée (guest panelist).
    #1: Miss Dana Craig (nightclub bouncer)
    #2: Frank Bisignano (cook on US Navy Blimp)
    #3: Dick Powell
    #4: Mrs. Natalie Carbone Mangini (atomic scientist)
    The cook successfully stumped the panel, but Francis correctly guessed the bouncer, while Kilgallen identified Powell and the scientist. By several accounts, Vallée appeared unfamiliar with the show, asking inane questions and appearing lost at times.

31. ***The Mike Wallace Interview,*** 1958, ABC
    Long before *60 Minutes*, Mike Wallace was a hard-edged investigative journalist. His program *Night-Beat* (1956-57) led to *The Mike Wallace Interview*. These 30-minute, primetime interviews with personalities ranging from Aldous Huxley to mobsters, William O. Douglas to Klansmen, earned him the nickname of "Mike Malice." Rudy Vallée appeared in 1958, along with other luminaries such as Peter Ustinov, Reinhold Neibuhr and Lili St. Cyr.

32. ***The Jimmy Dean Show,*** 1958, CBS Jimmy Dean (host/star), Joel Herron (associate producer, music director/pianist).
    Singer Jimmy Dean's variety shows have often been credited with popularizing country music. His 1957 daytime program, *The CBS Country Music Show*, went to primetime the next two years, and he returned for a third go-round for ABC from 1963-1966. Rudy Vallée made an appearance during the 1958 season.

33. ***The Red Skelton Show***, October 28, 1958, CBS Season 8 / Episode 5 episode: "Clem Sings." Red Skelton (star), Seymour Berns (director), Jan Arvan (Ferguson), Reed Hadley (district attorney), Isabel Randolph (Mrs. Witherspoon), Lennie Bremen (Nick).

Clem Kadiddlehopper (Red Skelton) claims to have a hidden musical talent designed to get himself some free singing lessons. Of course, knowing Clem, it only ends up in a hilarious tangle of fraud and plagiarism. Rudy Vallée and orchestra leader David Rose appear as themselves.

34. ***The Garry Moore Show***, 1959, CBS Garry Moore (host), Durward Kirby (regular), Howard Smith Orchestra (1958-59), Carol Burnett (1959-1962).

Genial Garry Moore hosted this variety of comedy, song and dance, monologues and interaction with the studio audience. The original hour-long series ran from September 30, 1958 to June 16, 1964, with a brief 4-month return in 1966-7. Introduced on the program were such stars-to-be as Carol Burnett, Jonathan Winters, Don Adams, Dorothy Loudon and Don Knotts, as well as old-time stars such as Rudy Vallée.

35. ***The George Gobel Show***, 1959, CBS George Gobel (star/host), Phyllis Avery (George's wife, Alice 1958-59), Anita Bryant, The Modernaires, Harry Von Zell (regulars 1959-60).

"Lonesome George" Gobel hosted three similar variety shows from 1954 to 1960. Opening with a monologue, and somewhere working in trademark sayings like "I'll be a dirty bird," Gobel presented performers such as Eddie Fisher, The Modernaires and Rudy Vallée (1959).

36. *The Perry Como Show,* November 15, 1961 Perry Como (host). Guest Stars: Rudy Vallée, Tommy Sands, Nancy Sinatra.

37. *What's My Line?,* November 26, 1961, CBS Season 13 / Episode 590 John Daly (moderator), Johnny Olson (announcer). Regular panelists: Arlene Francis, Bennett Cerf, Dorothy Kilgallen. with Darren McGavin (guest panelist).
#1: Mr. Kirpal Singh (rocket designer)
#2: Miss Carole Chamberlain (nightclub underwater act)
#3: Rudy Vallée (mystery guest)
Vallée used a disguised high squeaky voice in an attempt to fool the panel. Francis identified him however, the only correct guess of the evening. Rudy's appearance on this show was designed mainly to promote his current play, *How to Succeed in Business Without Really Trying.*

38. *The Ed Sullivan Show,* June 3, 1962, CBS Season 15 / Episode 710 (formerly *Toast of the Town*) Ed Sullivan (host), Art Hannes (announcer). Guest Stars: Rudy Vallée, Bill Dana (as José Jimenez), Peter Nero, Chita Rivera, Paul Anka ("A Steel Guitar and a Glass of Wine"), Dave Barry (comedian), Smaxie and Maxie (performing seals), Peg Leg Bates (tap dancer), Adam Keefe (comedian), Willie Mays (giving baseball tips, what else!).

39. *The Tonight Show Starring Johnny Carson*, October 1, 1962, NBC Season 1 / Episode 1 (Carson premiere show) Johnny Carson (host), Skitch Henderson (orchestra leader). Guest Stars: Joan Crawford, Rudy Vallée, Mel Brooks, The Phoenix Singers, Tony Bennett.
Rudy has the honor, though few would have guessed it at the time, of helping Johnny Carson inaugurate his 30-year run as the king of late-night television.

40. *Pantomime Quiz,* April 22, 1963 Season 2/Episode 59 Mike Stokey (host). Sebastian Cabot, Robert Clary, Beverly Garland, Ross Martin (regular panelists), with Rudy Vallée (guest panelist).

41. *What's My Line?,* July 5, 1964, CBS Season 15 / Episode 720 John Daly (moderator), Johnny Olson (announcer). Regular panelists: Arlene Francis, Bennett Cerf, Dorothy Kilgallen. With Rudy Vallée (guest panelist).
#1: Peter Gabel (guide at NYC World's Fair)
#2: Miss Joyce Ivey (mosquito species sorter)
#3: Sue Lyon (mystery guest)
Lyon failed to fool Kilgallen, but promoted her upcoming appearance in *The Night of the Iguana.* Both of the other guests were indeed mysteries to the panel, the wild joke being that Arlene Francis failed to recognize her own (and Martin Gabel's) son Peter!

42. *On Broadway Tonight,* July 8, 1964 to September 16, 1964, CBS, series host, variety-hour to introduce new talent, 60 minutes, color. Theme music composed by Robert Crewe, Jr., Robert Gaudio, Keefe Brasselle and performed by The Four Seasons; Irving Mansfield (producer).
Rudy Vallée hosted six acts, primarily of young and unknown talent, giving them their first exposure on national television. A few of the up-and-coming comedians who appeared during the series' short (1964-1965) run were Rich Little, Rodney Dangerfield and George Carlin.

43. *On Broadway Tonight,* January 1, 1965 to March 12, 1965, CBS, series host, (see #42 above)

44. *Where the Action Is,* February 9, 1967 Season 3 / Episode 419 episode: "The Sopwith Camel." Dick Clark (host, announcer), Paul

Revere and the Raiders (house band), Jimmy Hibbard (dancer), Keith Allison, Mark Lindsay, Linda Scott, Phil Volk, Eddie Rambeau, Tina Mason, Steve Alaimo, Drake Levin, Michael Smith (semi-regular singers). Guest Stars: The Sopwith Camel, Rudy Vallée.

45. *Batman,* November 23, 1967, ABC Season 3 / Episode 105 episode: "The Londinium Larcenies." Elkan Allen and Charles Hoffman (writers), Oscar Rudolph (director). Adam West (Bruce Wayne/Batman), Burt Ward (Dick Grayson/Robin), Alan Napier (Alfred Pennyworth), Yvonne Craig (Barbara Gordon/Batgirl), Stafford Repp (Chief O'Hara), William Dozier (narrator), David Lewis (Warden Crichton), Byron Keith (Mayor Linseed), Neil Hamilton (Commissioner James Gordon). Recurring roles: Maurice Dallimore (Watson), Monte Landis (Basil), Joe Abdullah (Fagin), Gil Stuart (the bobby). Guest Stars: Glynis Johns (Lady Penelope Peasoup), Rudy Vallée (Lord Marmaduke Ffogg), Lyn Peters (Prudence), Harvey Jason (Scudder), Larry Anthony (Digby), Aleta Rotell (Daisy), Nannette Turner (Sheila), Lynley Lawrence (Kit), Stacey Gregg (Rosamund).
Batman and Robin are called in to solve the mystery of missing antique snuffboxes, these having been stolen by Lord Marmaduke Ffogg (Rudy Vallée) and his sister Lady Penelope Peasoup (Glynis Johns).

46. *Batman,* November 30, 1967, ABC Season 3 / Episode 106 episode: "The Foggiest Notion."
Batman and Robin continue their pursuit of badguys Lord Ffogg (Vallée) and Lady Peasoup (Johns). After several near-fatal adventures, the dynamic duo corners Ffogg. But (since this is a 3-parter), the Lord escapes again in his man-made misty fog.

47. *Batman,* December 7, 1967, ABC Season 33 / Episode 107 episode: "The Bloody Tower"

Pursuing Lord Ffogg and Lady Peasoup, the duo ends up in a dungeon threatened by Ffogg's lethal fog pellets. Batman escapes, rescues a trapped Batgirl and together with Robin finally captures the Lord and Lady. Madge Blake appears in the finale, giving her final performance as Aunt Harriet Cooper.

48. *Death Valley Days,* September 27, 1967, Syndicated Season 16 / Episode 384 episode: "The Friend." Guest Stars: Robert Taylor, Rudy Vallée.

One of the longest-running Western series, originating on radio in the 1930s, this based-on-fact show was previously hosted by Ronald Reagan and sponsored by authentic Death Valley product "20 Mule Team" Borax.

49. *The Merv Griffin Show,* January 2, 1968, Syndicated Season 3 / Episode 57 Merv Griffin (host). Guest Stars: Hugh Downs, Paul Ford, David Susskind, Rudy Vallée.

Former big-band singer, talk-show host Griffin would later create mega-hits *Jeopardy* and *Wheel of Fortune.*

50. *Petticoat Junction,* December 27, 1969, CBS Season 7 / Episode 210 episode: "But I've Never Been in Erie, Pa." Edgar Buchanan ("Uncle Joe" Carson), Meredith MacRae (Billie Jo Bradley), Lori Saunders (Bobbie Jo Bradley), Linda Henning (Betty Jo Bradley),

Frank Cady (Sam Drucker), Mike Minor (Steve Elliott), June Lockhart (Dr. Janet Craig). Guest Stars: Rudy Vallée (H.A. Smith), Tim Graham (Bert).

Bea Benaderet starred as mother Kate Bradley until her death in 1968, to be replaced by June Lockhart as Dr. Craig, in this, one of the most popular rural comedies of the 1960s.

51. *The Name of the Game,* January 16, 1970, NBC Season 2 / Episode 42 episode: "Island of Gold and Precious Stones." Gene Barry (Glenn Howard), Susan Saint James (Peggy Maxwell), Anthony Franciosa (Jeff Dillon). Guest Stars: Keith McConnell (Finch), Mario Alcade (Alejandro), Doreen Lang (Miss March), Yvonne DeCarlo (Mrs. Levene), Lester Matthews (Porter), Michael Walker (Mark), Henry Jones (George), Lee Meriwether (Bridget), Edward Everett Horton (Basil Fletcher), Hazel Court (Miss L. Playfair), Irene Tsu (Miss Takashima), Estelle Winwood, Rudy Vallée (cameos).

52. *The Merv Griffin Show,* June 5, 1970 Season 5 / Episode 117 Merv Griffin (host). Guest Stars: Lillian Briggs, Tommy James, Julius LaRosa, Rudy Vallée.

53. *Here's Lucy,* November 30, l970, CBS Season 3 / Episode 60 episode: "Lucy and Rudy Vallée." Coby Ruskin (director), David Ketchum, Bruce Shelly (writers), Roy Rowan (announcer). Lucille Ball (Lucille Carter), Desi Arnaz, Jr. (Craig Carter), Gale Gordon (Harrison Otis), Lucie Arnaz (Kim Carter), Vanda Barra. Guest Stars: Rudy Vallée (himself), with Herbie Faye, Philip Vandervort, Marnelle Wright, Gloria Wood, George Bledsoe, Thomas D. Kenny, Mack McLean, Sue Allen.

54. *Preston Sturges: The Rise and Fall of an American Dreamer,* West German documentary, 1970, re-run for American TV in 1990 on the PBS *American Masters* Series. Interspersed with clips from many of Sturges' classic film moments, Hans C. Blumenberg (writer and director) interviews Eddie Bracken, Rudy Vallée and others who worked with Preston Sturges, giving us an interesting overview of the director's career.

55. *The Chicago Teddy Bears,* September 17, 1971, CBS Season 1 / Episode 1 episode: "Tender Loving Kindness." Jamie Farr (Lefty), Marvin Kaplan (Marvin), Art Metrano (Nick Marr), Mike Mazurki (July), John Banner (Uncle Latzi), Dean Jones (Linc), Huntz Hall (Dutch), Mickey Shaughnessy (Lefty Too). Guest Star: Rudy Vallée. In a brief appearance, Rudy helps kick off another (though short-lived) series by causing trouble between Nick and Linc.

56. *Night Gallery,* October 6, 1971, NBC Season 2 / Episode 31 episode: "Marmalade Wine." Jerrold Freedman (director and writer), based on Joan Aiken's short story "Marmalade Wine," originally published in the September 1958 issue of *Suspense Magazine.* Rod Serling (host). Guest Stars: Robert Morse (Roger Blacker), Rudy Vallée (Dr. Francis Deeking). Roger Blacker (Morse) unfortunately brags once too often, to a demented surgeon (Vallée). Result: both unpleasant and painful.

57. *Alias Smith and Jones,* November 18, 1971, ABC Season 2 /
Episode 25 episode: "Dreadful Sorry, Clementine." Barry Shear
(director), Glen Larson and John Thomas James (writers), Roger
Davis (narrator). Ben Murphy (Thaddeus Jones/Jed "Kid" Curry),
Pete Duel (Joshua Smith/Hannibal Heyes). Guest Stars: Keenan
Wynn (Horace Wingate), Rudy Vallée (Winford Fletcher),
Ken Scott (Toomey), Stuart Randell (Hawkins), Jackie Coogan
(Crawford), Don Ameche (Diamond Jim Guffy), Sally Field
(Clementine Hale). Amidst fellow old-time stars Wynn, Ameche
and Coogan, Vallée and Smith and Jones become involved in a
$50,000 swindle.

58. *Alias Smith and Jones,* January 20, 1972, ABC Season 2 / Episode
32 episode: "The Man Who Broke the Bank at Red Gap." Richard
Benedict (director), John Thomas James, Ronson Howitzer (writers),
Roger Davis (narrator). Ben Murphy (Thaddeus Jones/Jed "Kid"
Curry), Pete Duel (Joshua Smith/Hannibal Heyes), Ford Rainey
(Collins), Dennis Fimple (Kyle Murtry). Guest Stars: Richard Wright
(Billy), Rudy Vallée (Winford Fletcher), Bill Toomey (assistant), Joe
Schneider (Jess), Clarke Gordon (Sheriff McWhirter), Broderick
Crawford (Powers). Vallée returns in the role of Winford Fletcher
as Smith and Jones find themselves framed for bank robbery by an
embezzling banker. Their solution: obviously, arrange a second bank
robbery and clear their 'good' names. Star Pete Duel would appear
in only one more episode after this before his tragic suicide. His role
would be assumed by narrator Roger Davis.

59. *The Mike Douglas Show,* February 27, 1973 Episode 203.
Mike Douglas (host), Jay Stewart (announcer). Guest Stars:
Norm Crosby, Rudy Vallée.

60. *Ellery Queen,* March 7, l976, NBC Season 1 / Episode 20 episode: "The Adventure of the Tyrant of Tin Pan Alley." Seymour Robbie (director). David Wayne (Inspector Richard Queen), Jim Hutton (Ellery Queen), Tom Reese (Sergeant Velie), John Hillerman (Simon Brimmer). Guest Stars: Albert Salmi (Herbie Morrow), Polly Bergen (Dina Carroll-Wyner), Ken Berry (Buddy Parker), Michael Callan (Gary Swift), Norman Fell (Errol Keyes), Rudy Vallée (Alvin Wyner), Renne Jarrett (Penny Carroll), Brad David (Dan Murphy), Dori Brenner (Laura Schramm), Vince Howard (Charlie), Harold Ayler (engineer), Billy Varga (security guard). Plot for this episode was suggested by the payola scandals of the 1950s. In Hillerman's last appearance as the radio "sleuth," he keeps his batting average at .000 by again failing to correctly identify the killer and best Ellery. One of the most popular of literary detectives, this exceptionally well-done Queen series was unfortunately short-lived.

80th birthday at home with Dick Clark and Johnnie Ray. Photo by Yani Begakis

61. *The Muppets Go Hollywood,* May 16, 1979 Season 6 / Episode 131
Jim Henson, Frank Oz, Jerry Nelson, Richard Hunt, Dave Goelz,
Steve Whitmire, Kathryn Mullen (muppets). Dick Van Dyke,
Rita Moreno (hosts). Guest stars (alphabetically): Steve Allen,
Anne Bancroft, Candace Bergen, Mel Brooks, LeVar Burton, Gary
Busey, Red Buttons, Ruth Buzzi, James Coburn, Dom DeLuise,
Phyllis Diller, Charles Durning, Peter Falk, Louise Fletcher, John
Forsythe, James Frawley, Florence Henderson, Don Knotts, Cheryl
Ladd, Liberace, Steve Martin, Johnny Mathis, Ethel Merman,
Don Most, Richard Mulligan, Valerie Perrine, Vincent Price,
Christopher Reeve, Carl Reiner, Robert Stack, Jean Stapleton,
Maureen Stapleton, Rudy Vallée, Raquel Welch. A vehicle to plug
the Muppets' first movie, the plot being: "let's throw a party at the
Coconut Grove and invite everyone in Hollywood!"

62. *CHiPs,* January 20, 1979, NBC Season 2 / Episode 38 episode: "Pressure Point." Erik Estrada (Officer Francis "Ponch" Poncherello), Larry Wilcox (Officer Jon Baker), Robert Pine (Sgt. Joseph Getraer), Brianne Leary (Officer Sindy Cahill). Guest Stars: Mary Crosby (Chris), Douglas Fowley (Barney), Guy Stockwell (Paul Everett), Rudy Vallée (Arthur Forbinger), Tom Trouple (Darrell Justin), David Wiley (George Price), Michael Stearns (guard).

    This show about California motorcycle officers was a huge hit, particularly amongst teenage girls.

63. *The Perfect Woman,* 1981, movie for cable TV. Bob Emenegger (director). Cast: Joanne Nail (the perfect woman), Peter Kastner (Emo), Barry Gordon, Cameron Mitchell, Rudy Vallée, Marie Windsor, Fred Willard. Two inept subjects are sent to Earth by an alien king to find him a queen.

64. *Santa Barbara,* November 1984, NBC Season 1 / Episode 106 Jerome and Bridget Dobson (writers). Among the massive cast: Robert Brian Wilson (Channing Capwell, Jr.), Rupert Ravens (Danny Andrade), Stephen Meadows (Peter Flint). Rudy Vallée guest stars on this episode as an elderly convict. One of the better soaps, this would be Rudy's last live appearance on television.

65. *Hollywood, The Golden Years: The RKO Story,* 1987 6-part miniseries. Edward Asner (host, narrator), with (alphabetically): Fred Astaire, Lucille Ball, Pandro Berman, Joan Fontaine, Stewart

**At fund-raising party with Ellie and former
Mayor Sam Yorty. Photo by Yani Begakis**

Granger, Jane Greer, Katharine Hepburn, John Houseman, Howard
Hughes, Garson Kanin, Janet Leigh, Burgess Meredith, Ann Miller,
Robert Mitchum, Hermes Pan, Erik Rhodes, Ginger Rogers, Jane
Russell, Lili St. Cyr, Rudy Vallée, Fay Wray. A nostalgic look back at
the history of the great RKO studio, with interviews by many of the
stars who worked there. Not aired until 1987, Rudy Vallée died in
July 1986.

The Written Word
In His Own Words:

Books:

Vagabond Dreams Come True, E.P. Dutton & Company, N.Y., 1930.
My Time is Your Time (with Gil McKean), Ivan Obolensky, N.Y., 1962.
Let the Chips Fall, Stackpole Books, Harrisburg, Pa., 1975.
Rudy Vallée Kisses & Tells (pb version of *Let the Chips Fall*), Major Books, Canoga Park, Cal., 1976.
Al Lewis: *Rhymes to Riches*, preface and lengthy postscript by Rudy Vallée, Donaldson, Douglas & Gumble, Inc., N.Y., 1935.
Louis Armstrong: *Swing That Music*, preface by Rudy Vallée, Longmans, Green & Co., N.Y., 1936.

Articles/Interviews:

"The Dream and the Glory–John Adams," *Coronet*, July 1955.
"40 Years a Girl-Watcher," *Bachelor*, September 1962.
"I Stand By," *Pictorial Review*, August 1936.
"It's My Humble Opinion," *Radio Stars*, February 1937 through August 1938
"Rudy Vallée's Music Notebook," *Radioland*, January 1935.

Eleanor Vallée: *My Vagabond Lover*, Taylor Publishing Company, Dallas, Texas, 1996.

Favorite expression: "I don't know, I'm sure."

Ambition: "To run things."

"At times, when I begin to broadcast, I feel like a surgeon beginning to operate."

"Love grown cold is a bitter morsel."

"Our romance will last forever and ever and even longer."

"I certainly have no illusions about my personality or attractiveness."

"Our college kids are well informed about everything they don't have to study."

"I think those who will not be interested in me after my marriage will be insignificant in number."

"Certainly I am very far from perfect" (Zipser, Arthur and Novack, George: *Who's Hooey*, 1932)

BIBLIOGRAPHY:

Books:
Adams, Joey: *Laugh Your Calories Away – All-Star Recipes*, Cumberland Packing Corporation, 1970.

Alba, Ben: *Inventing Late Night – Steve Allen and the Original Tonight Show*, Prometheus Books, Amherst, N.Y., 2005.

Bearse, Ray (editor): *Maine – A Guide to the Vacation State*, Houghton Mifflin Company, Boston, 1969.

DeLong, Thomas A.: *The Mighty Music Box – The Golden Age of Musical Radio*, Amber Crest Books, Inc., Los Angeles, Ca., 1980.

___ *Radio Stars – An Illustrated Biographical Dictionary of 953 Performers, 1920 through 1960*, McFarland & Company, Jefferson, N.C., 1996.

Dunning, John: *Tune in Yesterday*, Prentice-Hall Inc., Englewood Cliffs, N.J., 1976.

Eichberg, Robert: *Radio Stars of Today*, L.C. Page & Company, Boston, Mass., 1937.

Ewen, David: *The Story of America's Musical Theater*, Chilton Book Company, Philadelphia, Pa., 1968.

Fetrow, Alan G.: *Feature Films, 1940-1949*, McFarland & Company, Jefferson, N.C., 1994.

___ *Sound Films, 1927-1937*, McFarland & Company, Jefferson, N.C., 1992.

Freman, Lauren: *The Record of Sigma Alpha Epsilon, SAE Fraternity*, Evanston, Illinois, March 1938.

Gray, Charleson: *The Vagabond Lover*, photoplay edition from the scenario by James Creelman, A.L. Burt Company, N.Y., 1929.

Gross, Ben: *I Looked & I Listened*, Arlington House, New Rochelle, N.Y.,1970.

Hart, Larry: *Did I Wake You Up?*, Riedinger & Riedinger Limited, Schenectady, N.Y., 1970.

Hayes, Richard K.: *Kate Smith*, McFarland & Company, Jefferson, N.C., 1995.

Henderson, Amy: *On the Air – Pioneers of American Broadcasting*, Smithsonian Institute Press, Washington, D.C. 1988.

Inman, David: *The TV Encyclopedia*, Putnam Publishing Group, N.Y., 1991.

Jackson, Stanley: *The Savoy*, Frederick Muller Ltd., London, 1965.

Ketover, Karen Sherman: *Westbrook, Maine Cemeteries*, Heritage

Books, Inc., Bowie, Md., 1996.

Kiner, Larry F.: *The Rudy Vallée Discography*, Greenwood Press, Westport, Ct., 1985, Discographies #15.

LeConte, Dianne and the Westbrook History 2000 Committee: *Westbrook on the Presumpscot*, Arcadia Publishing, Dover, N.H., 1996.

Lombardo, Guy (with Jack Altshul): *Auld Acquaintance*, Doubleday & Company, Garden City, N.Y., 1975.

Maltin, Leonard: *The Great American Broadcast*, Dutton Books, New York, 1997.

McCarthy, Albert: *The Dance Band Era*, Spring Books, London & N.Y., 1974.

Nachman, Gerald: *Raised on Radio*, Pantheon Books, N.Y., 1998. Oblak,

Oblak, John B.: *Bringing Broadway to Maine – The History of Lakewood, Maine*, Moore-Langen Printing & Publishing Co., Terre Haute, Indiana, 1971.

Post, Russell Lee (editor): *History of the Class of 1927 – Yale College*, Decennial Record, New Haven, Ct., 1938.

Walker, Leo: *The Wonderful Era of the Great Dance Bands*, Howell-North Books, Berkeley, Cal., 1964.

Zipser, Arthur and Novack, George: *Who's Hooey – Nitwitticisms of the Notable*, E.P. Dutton Incorporated, N.Y., 1932.

Articles:

Albert, Dora. "She Scooped the World" *Radio Guide*, February 20, 1937.

___ The Bachelor and the Bobby-Soxer, *Movie Story*, August 1947.

___ The Beautiful Blonde From Bashful Bend, *Movie Story*, July 1949.

Black, Susan. "Play Reviews" *Theatre Arts*, December 1961.

Paperback - New Title: *"Rudy Vallée Kisses and Tells"*

Boyne, George. "It's the Vallée Varieties Now, but Rudy Still Croons" *Record Weekly Magazine*, September 22, 1934.

Burrows, Abe. "How to Succeed in (Show) Business" *Show Business Illustrated*, January 23, 1962.

Christy, Earl (cover art). *Radio Stars*, May 1936.

Davenport, Dorothy. "The Vagabond Lover" *Screen Book*, March 1930.

___ "Do Radio Stars Earn Their Pay?" *Radio Stars*, July 1934.

Dudley, Fredda. "The Gentleman from Maine" *Silver Screen*, February 1945.

Dunn, Angela Fox. "Love Song" *Globe*, August 5, 1986.

Fenton, Maurice. "The Best Records from New Pictures" *Photoplay*, September 1930.

Fletcher, Adele Whitely. "At Last! The Truth about Fay and Rudy" *Radio Stars*, May 1934.

___ "What Freedom Cost Rudy Vallée" *Radio Guide*, June 13, 1936.

___ "For Entertainment's Sake" *Movie-Radio Guide*, August 15, 1941.

___ Gold-Diggers in Paris, *Screen Romances*, June 1938.

___ Happy Go Lucky, *Modern Screen*, April 1943.

Harrower, Jack. "For Husbands Only" *Cinema*, January 1930.

___ "He Was Grandma's Idol" TV *Guide*, August 22, 1964.

___ "Heard Regularly" What's *on the Air*, January 1931.

His former secretary. "What Rudy Vallée Never Told" *Radio Guide*, February 24, 1934.

___ I Remember Mama, *Movie Story*, May 1948.

Jamison, Jack. "Two Fists for Fame" *Radio Guide*, October 24, 1936.

___ "Jane Greer" *Life Magazine*, June 2, 1947.

J.C. "Rudy Vallée Gives a Breakfast Party" *Movie-Radio Guide*, November 7, 1941.

Kent, George. "Rah Rah Radio!" *Radio Stars*, January 1935.

Kutner, Nanette. "A Date with Rudy Vallée" *Radio Stars*, October 1936.

Lewis, Martin. "Airialto Lowdown" *Radio Guide*, July 9, 1938.

Lonsdale, Jeff. "The Naughty Nude Rudy Vallée Forgot to Remember" *Uncensored*, April 1956.

Matthews, Francis Barr. "Would You Want a Private or Public Wife?" *Radio Stars*, April 1934.

___ "Meet Rudy Vallée's Girl" *Screen Book*, September 1939.

Mitchell, Mrs. Curtis. "Heaven in the Pines" *Radio Stars*, November 1935.

___ The Palm Beach Story, *Photoplay combined with Movie Mirror*, January 1943.

___ People Are Funny, *Screenland*, January 1949.

___ "Pix Without Pose" *Screen Romances*, February 1945.

Plummer, Evans. "Hollywood Showdown" *Radio Guide*, November 27, 1937.

___ "Hollywood Showdown" *Radio Guide*, January 19, 1940.

___ "In Hollywood" *Movie and Radio Guide*, June 21, 1940.

___ "The Inside Story of the McCarthy Program Break-Up" *Radio Guide*, January 5, 1940.

___ "Plums and Prunes" *Radio Guide*, February 6, 1937.

Porter, Martin J. "What Price Music" *Radio Guide*, March 31, 1934.

___ "The Private Life of Rudy Vallée" *Look Magazine*, November 9, 1937.

___ "Radio Stars Turn Pirates" *Movie and Radio Guide*, July 5, 1940.

___ "A Real Record" *Radio Guide,* October 29, 1938.

___ "Rudy Vallée at Work" *Radio Guide*, January 9, 1937.

___ "Rudy Vallée Brings His 'Variety Hour' to NBC" *Radio Guide*, August 20, 1938.

___ "Rudy Vallée, Dog Fancier" *Movie and Radio Guide*, August 23, 1940.

___ "The Rudy Vallée-John Barrymore Show" *Movie-Radio Guide*, August 22, 1941.

___ "Rudy Vallée Raises His Voice" *Vanity Fair*, July 1929.

St. Johns, Adela Rogers. "The Private Life of Rudy Vallée" *Liberty*, April 7, 1934.

Scullin, George. "How to Succeed in Show Business by Being Rediscovered" *The Saturday Evening Post*, June 23, 1962.

Senseney, Dan. "What's New from Coast to Coast" *Radio Mirror*, July 1938.

___ So This is New York, *Movie Story*, March 1948.

Thomas, Lorraine. "Twelve Crowded Months" *Radio Guide*, January 12, 1940.

___ Unfaithfully Yours, *Screen Stories*, December 1948.

Vallée, Bill. "When Rudy Vallée Runs Away From it All" *Radio Mirror*, December 1934.

___ "Vocalists — Rudy Vallée," *Radio Album*, Spring 1942.

___ "'Vox Pop' Calling Rudy Vallée" *Movie-Radio Guide*, December 26, 1941.

Wald, Jerry. "I Know the Truth about Rudy Vallée's Strangest Feud" *Radio Mirror*, February 1938.

Wheeler, Dan. "What Are Rudy Vallée's Plans?" *Radio and Television Mirror*, November 1939.

Wilson, Shirley. "Rudy Vallée's Secret Passion" *Popular Songs*, March, 1935.

___ "X-Word Puzzle" *Radio Guide*, December 24, 1938.

What others had to say about Rudy:

"His kissing is as full of sanctity as the touch of holy bread." (High school classmates, presumably female)

"Rudy Vallée is God's gift to the American working girl." (Texas Guinan)

"I just adored him." (Rose Marie)

"Was tremendously impressed with meeting and working with this legend." (Alan Young)

"He was a lovely man." (Ann Miller)

Other material:

The Blue and White – Westbrook High School Yearbook, Volume IV -No. 1, June 1920.

Fleisher Yarns: Hand Knits for Men, as worn by NBC Radio Stars volume 62, 1940.

___ "Broadway—Rudy Valet" Comic section, *New York Daily News*, July 13, 1931.

___ "Fay Brands Vallée Wandering Lover" *Sunday News*, January 14, 1934.

___ *Ken Murray's Blackouts of 1944*, Souvenir Program, American

Offset Printers, L.A., 1944.

___ *Once Upon a Mattress*, Souvenir Program, Warren Letter Shop, 1973.

___ "Oust Student for Throwing Fruit at Rudy Vallée" *Dayton Daily News*, Dayton, Ohio, January 30, 1931.

___ *Radio Stars of Today*, National Union Radio Corporation, Art Gravure Corporation, N.Y.C., c.1931.

___ "Rudy Tells Public About Fay's 'Other Man'" *The Austin American*, Austin, Texas, January 13, 1934.

___ *Rudy Vallée's Love Songs*, Robbins Music Corporation, N.Y., 1934.

___ "Rudy Vallée Wins Divorce Point" *The Call Bulletin*, San Francisco, California, January 12, 1934.

___ "Sues Ruddy [sic] Vallée for $200,000" *Sapulpa Herald*, Sapulpa, Creek County, Oklahoma, December 23, 1929.

Wigler, Sam (editor): *Rudy Vallée and his Connecticut Yankees*, Souvenir Program, National Broadcasting Company combined concert and dance tour, Gordon Press, N.Y.C. 1930.

And:

Numerous assorted scrapbooks, clippings, and albums painstakingly and lovingly assembled by past unknown collectors and fans of Rudy Vallée.

Favorite recipe: Rudy Vallée's Lemon Lime Pie

(Crust): Beat two egg whites until stiff. Add two tablespoons powdered milk and beat. Add one teaspoon vanilla, pinch salt and two packets Sweet 'N Low. Bake at 275-300 degrees for 20 to 25 minutes.

(Filling):
    1 package lemon flavored dietetic gelatin,
    1 package lime flavored dietetic gelatin, 1/8 teaspoon salt,
    1 1/2 cups boiling water, 1/2 cup cold water,
    1 cup evaporated skim milk, green food coloring (optional).

Chill small bowl and beaters. Chill evaporated milk in ice cube tray until ice crystals begin to form. Combine lemon and lime gelatin, salt and boiling water. Add few drops food coloring, if desired. Chill until thickened but not set. In the chilled bowl, whip evaporated milk until it is stiff and holds a peak. Fold in gelatin mixture lightly but thoroughly. Turn into meringue shell. Chill at least three hours before serving. Serves 6- 8. (Adams, Joey: *All-Star Recipes*, 1970)

(On the secret of his success):

"Even with my God-given sense of rhythm and flair for phrasing I wouldn't have amounted to anything if I hadn't worked hard. When I was a boy, I washed the windows in my father's drugstore in Maine. When the clerks washed the windows they only washed the middle. When I washed them, I cleaned up all the soap powder in the corners. Those clerks are still in Maine.

And when I went to college, while the other boys were loafing or going to football games, I studied. When I would stand in line waiting to see the Dean, I would have a book in my hand. So with my chosen life-work. From the time I determined to become a great saxophone player I practiced five, six and seven hours a day.

People speak of luck. Luck may get you to the top for a moment, but it won't keep you there. Sometimes I go backstage and find the boys from my band reading detective stories. It makes me sad. What will happen to them in the future if they don't improve their minds? They should read books like *Strategy in Handling People*. They should try to improve their memories by associating telephone numbers, for instance with the date of the Civil War.

Summing up, remember, find your niche and then work hard. You must analyze yourself analytically and then put into your work what you expect to get out of it. The day has but twenty-four hours and we need all of them. Let us try to improve our minds every minute by studying our jobs. We have no time to waste if we would succeed." (Zipser, Arthur and Novack, George: *Who's Hooey*, 1932)

Index

I

Printed in the United States
206910BV00002B/1-3/P

9 781593 931407